TWENTIETH CENTURY PORTRAITS

RENOIR: Mme. Tilla Durieux, 1914. Oil, 36½ x 29″. Collection Stephen C. Clark, New York.

20th century PORTRAITS

BY MONROE WHEELER

THE MUSEUM OF MODERN ART • NEW YORK

CONTENTS

ACKNOWLEDGMENTS

The director of the exhibition wishes to thank the following for their invaluable counse and cooperation:

Miss Ines Amor, Mr. Walter C. Arensberg, Mr. R. Kirk Askew, Jr., Mr. Alfred H. Barr, Jr., Mr. W. McCormick Blair, Mrs. Adelyn D. Breeskin, Mr. André Breton, Mr. Frank Crown-nshield, Mr. Jimmy Ernst, Mrs. Willard Burdette Force, Mr. Douglas Fox, Mr. Lincoln Kirstein, Miss Antoinette Kraushaar, Mrs. Howard Linn, Miss Elizabeth McCausland, Mr. A. Hyatt Mayor, Mr. Russell A. Plimpton, Mr. Daniel Catton Rich, Mr. Charles H. Sawyer, Mr. Daniel Shatt, Mr. James Thrall Soby, Dr. W. R. Valentiner.

For special research and assistance: Miss Amy Abraham, Mrs. C. S. Hartman, Miss Margaret Miller, Miss Frances Pernas, Mr. Glenway Wescott.

MONROE WHEELER

LENDERS TO THE EXHIBITION

TWENTIETH CENTURY PORTRAITS

TERMS AND LIMITATIONS

"Portrait painting is a reasonable and natural consequence of affection," said Dr. Johnson, and although one may smile at so simple and downright an affirmation, it is amazing to find how true it is in our century. For it does seem that, for the most part, good artists portray only their own families and close friends. Even the specialists in portraiture have often done their best work when there happened to be some intimacy between them and the sitter, or at least some mutual enthusiasm. And many artists now refuse to undertake any prearranged painting of strangers at all.

This may be one reason why the illustrious men and women of today do not often go to our best artists for their portraits. There are exceptions: Clemenceau sat to both Manet and Rodin, Paula Modersohn-Becker painted the poet Rilke, Boldini painted Verdi; and a number of more recent and very impressive combinations are to be found in this volume. But it is unfortunately true that the portrayal of the great of the world by the great in art is very rare today, and it is hoped that some clarification of the nature of portraiture in our time may lead to an increase of it.

Portraiture as considered here means any representation of an individual known to the artist personally in which the appearance and character of that individual have been an important factor in his mind as he worked. This is a flexible rule, with endless gradations and deviations according to the artist's talent and thought. The line we can draw by means of it, as to what is a portrait and what is not, will seem arbitrary in certain instances. One can only suggest, here and there, what lies on one side and what on the other.

Now and then the distinction can be made in a sequence of pictures by one painter using the same model. There are several such sequences by Picasso, for example, some of them certainly portraits, so entitled and named, while others proceed to a quite impersonal idealization or abstraction.

There has been also, particularly in the United States, a great deal of figure painting which is not portraiture. The model may have been under the painter's scrutiny every day but he or she as an individual has meant nothing to him. His purpose has been pure painting; that is, attitude and atmosphere, line and color and volume. This may be as fine a thing as portraiture, or finer, but it is not the subject of the present study. Its exclusion, however, cannot be absolute because the categories of art sometimes overlap.

What people look like, and what can be made of their looks in the various techniques of drawing, painting and sculpture, is the problem, and there is no limit to the solutions or approaches. One need not, however, in judging portraits as art, require any conformity to the sitter's own view of his appearance. His requirements in this respect, of course, may be another matter. In the United States, it is amusing to note, the law is on the sitter's side. If, in commissioning a portrait, he has specified that it is to be a likeness acceptable to himself, and when the work is done he finds it unsatisfactory, he cannot be obliged to pay for it.

But it would be wrong to encourage the commissioning of portraits in any such vain, susceptible spirit, with a preconception derived from what the sitter has seen in the mirror, or a sense of inferiority, or from the flattery of others. It is a remunerative kind of art, and artists need remuneration; but very few of the good ones seem eager to undertake it, precisely because they dread the judgments of the subject and his family and friends. The artists, in fact, need more encouragement than the potential sitters. It is hoped that the present selection may make portraiture appeal to both artists and art lovers who have been indifferent to it.

If there is to be a revival of portraiture, certainly it should be based on appreciation of art, for art's sake, not on anyone's fond hope of flattery. It is an expensive type of art; it takes time as well as money, and the client who does not insist upon anything in particular will get better art for his trouble and expenditure. But if he really cares more for a certain set opinion of himself than for art, there is scarcely an artist alive whom he can trust. There never have been many; and even the best photographers do not always give satisfaction to vanity.

Our concern, then, is with the artist's notion of the appearance of the sitter, not the sitter's notion. Resemblance is the point of portraiture, to be sure, but it may be remoteness of resemblance, as well as closeness. The artist who departs the farthest from the mirror viewpoint, in extravagance or stylization of his art, sometimes is most keenly concerned with the individual appearance. His very keenness and enthusiasm may prompt a harsh image, unreal color and powerful, unflattering form. This is a realm of art in which the subject must somehow engage in the act of imagination along with the artist and run the risks of creation, too. And he may well consider it an exciting privilege thus to partake in the development of the art of his time.

As to the nature of this development, there is a saying of Pascal which Gustave Moreau used to quote to his pupils, among others Matisse and Rouault: "Human knowledge is like a sphere continually increasing, so that the larger the volume of it, the greater the number of points of contact with the unknown." Modern art in its actual productions having been so various, this is perhaps the only sound sense in which to define its principle. As a whole it differs from previous art only in one respect, and various extremes of it are reconcilable only in one characteristic, namely: that it entails a belief not in any single specific standard of excellence or established method, but in experiment and exploration always, with a view to further development of the canon of beauty beyond the range of any artist's ability at a given moment, and further and further beyond towards the unknown.

In the Renaissance this was taken for granted as the nature of creative art; it went hand in hand with experimental science. The true age-old tradition is to keep departing from what seems traditional, on and on into the future, in which sense the legitimacy even of the extreme moderns cannot be denied, whether or not one admires them.

The purpose of this brief survey is simply to distinguish and illustrate the feeling of the chief artists of the twentieth century about this one subdivision of art, to review the story of art in our time in terms of portraiture, and to suggest a certain broadening of the meaning of the word "portrait" to include works of a freer imagination, so that the painter and sculptor need no longer shrink from it or neglect it and so that the potential sitter will cease to expect what there is no likelihood of his getting from a good artist. For purposes of contrast and comparison there have been included, without illusion, a few works of art less original in spirit and pictorial method than the majority of the selections. A number of photographs also are shown, for in judging a portrait some familiarity with the looks of the sitter is important, especially if the departure from reality in the artist's idiom is extreme in any way.

In many cases more than one portrait of the same sitter will be found, as well as photographs, to permit deduction of his appearance in reality and to show how various the approaches to the problem of portrayal may be. These groups may also serve as a basis for direct comparison of the esthetics and techniques of the artists in question. There are assorted likenesses of Mlle. Olivier, Mme. Lipchitz, Mrs. Dale, Miss Bonney and Miss Lloyd, and of Mr. Kirstein (pages 48, 49, 66, 67, 79, 81, 103, 118 and 119); and there are numerous pairs of portraits in various media which appear in good contrast and give direct instruction about our subject.

It is discouraging, and at the same time gratifying, to think that any such selection of works of art can only stir the surface of a great obscure treasure and remind everyone of something he knows which others may not know. This is especially true where portraiture is concerned because it is a personal kind of possession, less frequently offered for sale or exhibited than any other.

EAKINS AND THE EIGHT

EAKINS was well past middle age when the century began and by that time he had become a professional portraitist. But his career was not a happy one. Perhaps his spirit was not aggressive enough, perhaps the burden of a puritanical and plutocratic society in those days was greater than we can now imagine. Much of his work was somber, and for various reasons his influence upon the art of the beginning of the century was a little retardatory. His own studies in Europe were rather dull and academic, with Gérôme and Bonnat, and he returned to Philadelphia to teach for a living, which, as it turned out, was more unfortunate still.

His insistence upon teaching from the nude model aroused the Philadelphians to bring pressure upon him to resign, which he did in 1886. He had been wonderfully successful with his pupils, who picketed the Academy with large E's for Eakins on their hats. But it was hopeless, and we know from his correspondence that he felt the confusion and melancholy of this experience all the rest of his life.

After that he painted chiefly portraits, more of them than he liked; and they appear to us now to be the very spirit of Philadelphia personified; scientists, prelates, austere gentlemen and great ladies. He gave them a prosaically truthful aspect, stiff simplicity of attitude and dark colors, and as he was highly sensitive to the character as well as the appearance of his sitters, this severity of his art may have been inspired by them. In certain work of his old age, especially that which he never quite finished (page 33), there appears a more spirited expression and freer handling than in the paintings of the middle period.

His pupil Anshutz took his classes at the Academy and evidently continued the master's teaching very faithfully. Henri, Glackens, Luks and Sloan all studied with him. Later on they came to New York and joined four others in the group known as "the Eight." Their program together was a kind of reaction against Europe on the one hand and against the vulgar upper crust of our own new plutocracy on the other; a stay-at-home nationalism and an anti-aristocratic realism.

Glackens, Luks and Sloan had all worked as newspaper illustrators in Philadelphia in their youth and probably derived their interest in the passing show of everyday American life from this experience. Their program made them famous for a while. Oddly enough, the date of their first exhibition together, 1908, is the same as that generally given for the beginning of cubism. They were never so heartily hated as the rebels in France, but on the other hand they did not benefit by any rebound of the general taste as the French did.

Many of the portraits of HENRI seem today rather rude in execution, negative in color. But in felicitous examples, such as "The Masquerade Dress" (page 45), we find an artistry comparable to Whistler's; a little less refined but, on the other hand, less affected. LUKS was a great experimenter and his way of painting was uneven, but he had a considerable range of imagination and his impetuous style was his best (page 82).

GLACKENS was the finest painter of the group. Towards the end of his life he painted in soft, vivid colors which some of his contemporaries deplored, attributing them to the influence of Renoir. He had a sense of fashion as well as scene, and his large conversation piece of his wife and family conveys an extraordinary impression of the life of its time (page 47). SLOAN seems to have preferred groups to single portraits, and the intellectual or bohemian life is well suggested by the Corcoran Gallery's famous group of the elder Yeats with himself, his wife, and the respective authors of *I Have a Rendezvous with Death* and *The Flowering of New England* (page 46). BELLOWS was a younger man than any of these; he was Henri's pupil; and in the course of his successful career we see the dullness of pigment vanish. Like Glackens he gave up the somber colors inherited from Eakins and turned to brilliant tonality. The genre subjects became dramatic, even theatrical, and a formality almost in the manner of the eighteenth century developed in his portrait painting. He left a great amount of portraiture, especially of his beautiful wife and his daughter Jean (page 90).

LATE IMPRESSIONISM

The aged RENOIR seems not to have paid much attention to the extremes of modernism developing around him, and in spite of a certain reverence the young innovators of Paris were not particularly influenced by him. He had been through a conscious, radical reform of his own art in the 'eighties, and went on from it, closer to Cézanne than before, experimenting a little with sculpture, achieving at last in luminous, tremulous paint an almost sculptural form.

He had always done portraiture, a great deal of it, in fact, in his young manhood, quite successfully; and if his farsighted dealers, Durand-Ruel, had not sensed his greatness and guaranteed him a certain independence, his art might have been enslaved in a sequence of tedious commissions. They emancipated him, but apparently he liked people and enjoyed portrait painting, and did it until the end. He had great fame abroad by the turn of the century, especially in Germany, where he seemed to personify France.

Mme. Tilla Durieux, an actress of note, married to the Berlin picture-dealer Cassirer, sat to Renoir, and this glowing and serene likeness (frontispiece) may have consoled her in her womanly pride for certain indignities of portrayal to which the German expressionists had submitted her. There is a lithograph of her by Kokoschka, with loose features and a frightening gaze, and a bust by Barlach which is a nobler image though blunt and Gothic.

In the summer of 1910, when Renoir was sixty-nine years old and half crippled, he journeyed to Munich under agreement to paint several members of a great family named Thurneyssen. They met him at the railroad station with a guard of honor and a brass band. The formal portrait of Frau Thurneyssen with her daughter on her knee is a masterpiece (page 42). He did not succeed in fulfilling his entire contract that year, so the next year they sent their son to Cagnes to pose as a Greek shepherd.

From VUILLARD and BONNARD have come that last development of nineteenth-century art sometimes called "intimism." Vuillard is the finer portraitist, as may be seen in the early sensitive likeness of his brother-in-law, the painter Roussel (page 40), and in the famous later portrait of Théodore Duret (page 43).

Duret, as the first literary champion of the impressionists and Whistler's friend, was a celebrity in the art circles of Paris. Gertrude Stein tells of meeting him one day in Vollard's gallery, where Roussel was complaining of his failure and that of his friends to get portrait commissions. Duret looked at him kindly. "My young friend," he said, "there are two kinds of art, never forget this, there is art and there is official art. How can you, my poor young friend, hope to be official art?

Just look at yourself. Supposing an important personage came to France, and wanted to meet the representative painters and have his portrait painted. My dear young friend, just look at yourself, the very sight of you would terrify him. You are a nice young man, gentle and intelligent, but to the important personage you would not seem so, you would be terrible. . . You can see that you would not do. So never say another word about official recognition, or if you do, look in the mirror and think of important personages. No, my dear young friend, there is art and there is official art, and there always has been and there always will be."

Whistler's portrait of Duret appears in the background of Vuillard's, and it would take pages to explain as much of the difference between the nineteenth century and the twentieth in art as the comparison of these two portraits suggests at a glance. Whistler seemed a radical artist in his day; Vuillard never did; and one might expect their pictorial idioms to overlap, but they do not. Duret's character is clear and consistent in both pictures, with the lapse of thirty years between; only the eye of the painter has shifted and the taste of the time has changed.

Bonnard, whom connoisseurs such as Meier-Graefe have called the greatest living artist, achieved this fame by a gentle obstinacy in his own vein of impressionism, verging on abstract pattern. Now and then he has done great portraiture; very little of it has ever come outside the homes of certain grand-bourgeois in France and Switzerland. The strange, melancholy face of his wife peers out from the enchanting patchwork of light and shade in many of his famous canvases, such as "The Checkered Dress" (page 44).

THE SCHOOL OF PARIS

PICASSO surely is one of the strangest characters and one of the strongest talents in the whole history of art. His burning energy and restless intellect are apparent even in his early work, which is still derivative in style and gently romantic in spirit. The peculiar pattern of his genius appeared in his youth. Roughly speaking, it is this: with a simple, true impression as his point of departure he proceeds away from it in a series of variations and inventions, step by step, until the initial inspiring reality has vanished at last in intellectual enigma and pure form, unnatural or unrecognizable.

The enchantment of a particular face entered into Picasso's esthetic from the start, which is exemplified in his early blue period by a fine series of canvases inspired by a girl named Alice.

Then Picasso, struck by sudden admiration of Cézanne and a sculptural feeling for form, tried sculpture and began to experiment with an extreme third dimension in his painting as well. His model then was a beauty almost the exact antithesis of Alice: the dreamily inexpressive and classic Fernande Olivier. Once more Picasso, beginning with a direct and affectionate likeness, set about varying and analyzing and metamorphosing it. One of the busts of Fernande is a faithful three-dimensional version of the drawings (pages 48 and 49); but even in the abstract "Woman's Head" her noble arc of eyebrow, her haughty nose, her strong upper lip and chin evidently suggested the unflattering pattern in bronze. The entire development of his cubism came under the aegis of Fernande's classic good looks.

As he has nearly always been under the spell of one of these basic images, and developing it in some way, he naturally never cared to make a regular practice of portraiture, although as early as 1906 he produced one of the great modern likenesses, the portrait of Gertrude Stein (page 52). By the sitter's account it took ninety sittings and then, after an absence, he painted in the face from memory, in one day. At the time the resemblance was not thought to be close, but as sometimes happens in portraiture, it has seemed to intensify with the passage of the years, especially as to the expression and the posture.

One of the major works of analytical cubism is the large portrait of the picture-dealer Kahnweiler. The hardy good looks of the co-founder of cubism, Braque, inspired another good stylization on a smaller scale. There is very little likeness in either of these; but in certain other canvases, especially the portrait of Vollard as we compare it with Brassaï's photograph twenty-five years later (page 51), it is astonishing what a close resemblance Picasso was able to achieve by means of nothing but multiple facets; as recognizable as a photograph, and with lively expression interspersed somehow between the lines.

About 1917 his revolutionary ardor in art seemed to abate for a while in that classic period which may be associated once more with the beauty of one woman, this time his wife (page 84). He took the most conventional Greco-Roman ideal and handled it this way and that way with his powerful formal sense and his usual audacity. This, too, began with personal portraiture almost in the manner of Ingres and gradually turned to pictorial idealism and generalization, the "Woman in White" for example; and at last this likeness vanished, too, in large decorative compositions like mural painting, with no human particularity left.

Mlle. Dora Maar, who posed for the latest series of these metamorphoses, might feel that her fate in art had been the hardest of all. Her turn to inspire Picasso has been what is called his surrealist period, and now his hard imagination goes like clockwork, spellbound still, like a young man's imagination, but with not a trace of flattery (page 117). We should not recognize some of the images he has made of Dora Maar had he not repeated the shapes of her face, of the chair-back behind her and the hat on her head exactly as they appear in drawings bearing her name. Thus composers often take a simple theme, sweet folksong or chorale, and then astound the ear with its possibilities, winding and unwinding, masking and unmasking the original notes; and someone has compared Picasso's metamorphosed portraits to Beethoven's Diabelli variations.

Among other things, when so inclined, Picasso is a great draughtsman, for which he is revered even by those of the younger generation of artists who regard his type of modernism as a blind alley and are turning away from it. Oddly enough, the best of his drawing is simple portraiture. He has a passion for classic art, but, unwilling to imitate it, he has given most of his linear compositions with rather Greek figures a certain deliberate gawkiness. In portraiture, on the other hand, none of this embarrassment or mannerism ever comes between him and the subject. Sometimes the likeness is a little remote and ideal, sometimes it is clever, critical; and now and then, as in the full-length figure of Dr. Claribel Cone (page 85), he ranks with Ingres.

The temperament of MATISSE is in striking contrast to Picasso's. The friends of their youth were much impressed by this, and tried to derive a clarification of the modern movement from a kind of confrontation of them and from argument about them, if not between them. Matisse seemed the more rational, but from the start he had determined that the themes of his art were to be emotional and sensuous. Picasso had a burning and self-infatuated spirit; the problem of art aroused him no less than the attachments and disappointments of his private life, and yet he chose to make intellectual decisions about painting and to work according to them, going to every extreme he could think of.

Zervos tells us that one day Matisse conscientiously visited Picasso's studio in the Rue Ravignon to try to make up his mind about his friend's new methods.* Picasso showed him a cubist portrait and inquired whether he could make out the subject of it. Matisse admitted that he could not. Picasso then took a false moustache and placed it where it belonged amid the obscure angles and facets, and with that as a point of reference the

* Christian Zervos, *Cahiers d'Art*, Nos. 5 and 6.

elder painter succeeded in locating the other features, eyes, nose and necktie.

Picasso went on to explain that, as far as he was concerned, he wanted to get away from nature. The false moustache served as a key to all those analogies of form of which the cubist picture consisted; it guided the mind back to what his artistry had started with. But what interested him in art was what he could arrive at, not his inspiration or point of departure. This did not convince Matisse of the rightness of the cubist principle. He felt that pigment on a canvas ought to convey the vision of the artist without so much proof or external demonstration.

If we survey the entire range of contemporary portraiture, we are inclined to think that Matisse has an amazing gift for it. He has always been unwilling to be regarded as a portrait painter and yet, especially in the early decades of his art, he had a lively desire to paint portraits, independently, for his own pleasure. Many of these portraits pretend to be mere figure-compositions, with noncommittal titles; but they are really powerful likenesses of his wife ("The Woman with a Hat," page 53) and children, and certain pupils and collectors of his work.

As his teacher, Gustave Moreau, told him when he was young, his mission in painting was to simplify it. In an essay entitled "Notes of a Painter"* he himself stated the principle of his simplification very well, with tacit reference to portraiture:

"Expression to my way of thinking does not consist of the passion mirrored upon a human face or betrayed by a violent gesture. The whole arrangement of my picture is expressive . . . ."

He goes on to praise Egyptian art, animated in spite of its stiff immobility, and Greek art, calm even in the portrayal of violent movement, which, he adds, "the sculptor will have abridged and condensed, so that balance is re-established." He

*First published in La Grande Revue, Paris, December, 1918; translated and reprinted in its entirety in Henri-Matisse, The Museum of Modern Art, 1931.

uses the word "condensed" more than once in these brilliant pages, and when we turn from them to his portraits we see his formulating, summarizing, essential genius at work. He takes the multiplicity of details of physiognomy which we unconsciously bear in our minds as likeness, and powerfully molds them together into a kind of mask or icon which we never forget. Certainly no false moustache is needed to guide the eye to a comprehension of this kind of resemblance.

It takes the senses by surprise and by force. The fine portrait of Mlle. Landsberg (page 55), although it was painted several years after his colloquies with Picasso on cubism, shows some trace of the abstract preoccupation which, for the most part, Matisse declined to enter into.

Nothing ever seems to go to waste in the career of this great, tranquil craftsman, with a sense of his own destiny as strong as steel from beginning to end.

His sculpture is more satisfactory than Picasso's; it is perhaps closest to Rodin's, but more intensely condensed and restrained from the least seduction. Occasional pieces, slight and rather harsh in style though they seem, have unforgettable character (page 54), and are suggestive of that synthesis of sculpture and picture which most of the early modern artists seem to have had in mind.

MODIGLIANI was the only one of the famous first generation of modernism in Paris who specialized in portraiture or cared a great deal for it, but most unprofessionally, for he rarely if ever had what might be called a proper commission. His career of art, like his whole life, was disorderly in the extreme and very brief. His best inspiration came all crowded into the last two or three years of dissipation and illness. He began with sculpture, as to which Brancusi encouraged and advised him; and when he perfected his pictorial style it was like his sculpture in a way, somewhat in Brancusi's way—with an extreme simplification and elongation like Ivory Coast sculpture, to which he added out of his Italian inheritance some sweetness and

15

slight mannerism and display of color, reminiscent of the Sienese of the fifteenth century and of Botticelli.

He was an Italian Jew, proud of his supposed descent from Spinoza, a man of good education, fine physique and great charm. His comrades of Montmartre and Montparnasse all loved him, in spite of his vices and his temper, and he returned their affection, although he was not to be counted on for anything. His art was a rapid, almost daily record of the intimacies of the studio and the café: portraits of fellow-artists such as Lipchitz (page 66), portraits of beauties ephemerally well-known in the artist-quarter, such as Lolotte (color plate facing page 68), and occasionally a nude in an idle monumental attitude, all golden and red-golden. Perhaps because of the feverish rapidity of his execution—a canvas every few days, at the last—there is a look of family relationship about them all, especially the women. But they are subtle as well as decorative. In little touches everywhere there is acute characterization. For the *vie de Bohème* of the early century they constitute a gallery at least as various and revealing as the portraiture the Clouets did at the court of the Valois.

Modigliani sold his work as fast as he did it for the momentary satisfaction of his hunger or his thirst. In the 'twenties, in what appears to have been a speculators' market, it rose to extraordinarily high prices and then fell; and a more general popularity is probably still to come. His case is a little like the case of van Gogh and he reminds one also of Verlaine: inexcusable weakness of character with strength only for art. His art charms and then it cloys, but when one has accepted its limitations the charm works again.

Another notable figure of the tragic Bohemia of Paris, SOUTINE, who was Modigliani's close friend, did not quite evolve his individual art or achieve a real success until a decade later. In France he has been a lonely figure without any sort of group affiliation; in Germany he certainly would have been called an expressionist. Disdainful of the bourgeois and all its old self-flattering habits, he would hate to be regarded as a portrait painter but that, too, is a point of his pride and a matter of terminology. His usual sitters have been domestic servants and peasants, nameless. But again and again he has painted them in the classic poses of portraiture, simply seated or standing, facing him and facing us, and he decidedly characterizes and individualizes them.

The subject of the exceptional portrait we have reproduced is the wife of his chief patron and collector for many years (page 89). It is what must be called an unflattering likeness but it shows many of the qualities which have led art lovers, especially in France, to think him a great artist: the vehement statement of personal vision, the burning and palpable color, the directness of design, the almost awe-inspiring earnestness. All his painting, even when his subject is a woman of the world, is full of a feeling for the distress and the innocent ugliness of poor humanity. In their faces he finds the same kind of travail that appears in his stormy old trees and tumbledown walls, the same bright flesh that is in his still-lifes of the butcher shop, the same energy of nature that he displayed in his early flower pieces.

ROUAULT, the greatest living painter of the emotional or expressionist kind, really is not a portrait painter, and the distinction between him and Soutine in this respect is worth making. Soutine dwells on the personalities of his lowly men and women; he dramatizes their oddity and their loneliness; he thinks of them as important but misunderstood. Whereas Rouault is thinking not of people but of humankind, with a general compassion, a feeling of equal universal guilt, and according to this thought he creates a mask, a set of masks. His imagination is based upon the Christian faith, which is a great leveler or equalizer. The mask is something he has seen in his mind's eye and if one is baffled by it the best clue is to be found in his prose poems. "You think of me as a man of today," he says. "But I am not a man of today. I am a man of the time of the cathedrals."

Nevertheless he has painted portraits now and then. The large one of the painter Lebasque is one of the best (page 69). It must be strange to own a portrait of one's self by this master, to have before one, so to speak, a very probable likeness of one's immortal soul. A comparison of the four portraits of Miss Bonney shows his intense, exclusive spirituality very clearly (page 81). Lurçat gives us a worldly and decorative figure, Dufy an amusing, affectionate likeness; whereas the relation between somber color and strong design in Rouault's image of her is like something in theology. The profile portrait is painted on both sides of a translucent paper and mounted between two panes of glass, so that if it is properly placed the light of day animates it like an ancient window.

SELF-PORTRAYAL

Expressionism in Germany was generally conceived as intense self-expression; at any rate it has been so interpreted. But the tormented draughtsmanship and loose color of KOKOSCHKA have often served to express a dramatic perception of the emotional element in the lives and faces of others. Even in his youth he was a first-rate portrait painter. His self-portraits also show a kind of objectivity. It has been called a psychoanalytical art, which, of course, is a loose term, but there is profound analysis in these compelling pictures (pages 62 and 63).

Another brilliant artist of this generation, Max BECKMANN, who painted many handsome, somewhat caricatural portraits, is more famous for an extraordinary series of self-portraits. It suggests that he regards life as a play or rather a series of plays, casting himself in one role and then another; in our illustration he is a sailor (page 72). By his own account a philosophical principle underlies this self-portraiture. For the ego, as he said in a lecture in London in 1938, "is the great

veiled mystery of the world. Its path is, in some strange and peculiar manner, our path, and for this reason I am immersed in the phenomenon of the individual . . . What are you? What am I? These are the questions that constantly persecute and torment me and perhaps also play some part in my art."

Kaethe KOLLWITZ, beloved everywhere in the world for her humanitarian lithographs, also portrayed herself from year to year in sculpture as well as her customary black-and-white. It is not a histrionic self-portrayal like Beckmann's but rather a biography, pathetic, chapter by chapter, with the gradual touches of age and the traces of her compassion in a tragic era (page 73).

Self-portraiture, which these and many other Germans practiced with fanatical interest, corresponds to that absorption in problematic psychology which has been noted in Kokoschka's case. Without insisting upon any direct connection it may be remarked that the modern school of psychology is Germanic in origin and that it, too, is introspective and confessional. The self-exhibiting impulse of artists is far more than vanity. The inclination to boast of what they are or were, their playful desire to imagine what else they might have been, are only a part of it. Their concern often is rather to distinguish between opposite facets of personality, which they feel in conflict or which seem irreconcilable. One of our well-known though humble American artists, Vincent CANADÉ, has painted a remarkable series of this type of self-portrait (page 76). But in the more recent of these, to quote Guy Eglinton, "his modesty gives place to alternate arrogance and self-accusation . . . There is no end to the roles for which he casts himself. In the famous "Double Self-Portrait (Sunday and Monday)" he is the complete degenerate. Himself, he styles it, as he is and as he would like to be, though which is which God knows, so desperate are the faces which scowl out of that magnificent canvas."*

* Creative Art, July, 1928.

There is another fine example of American self-portraiture somewhat similar in spirit, a spirit divided against itself obscurely, by a man who should be considered with reference to the school of Paris and its influence upon our art. Alfred H. MAURER, the son of a nineteenth-century painter well-known for his racing pictures reproduced by Currier and Ives, distinguished himself at an early age by a vigorous realism not unlike the portraits of Henri and Luks. "The Black Parasol" is typical of the work of his youth (page 34): the tradition of Hals and the Spanish old masters somewhat brought up to date by the influence of Whistler, with a charming homespun American aspect all Maurer's own. Then he went to Paris and nothing came of the career which had seemed so simple and certain in his native land. The work of Matisse impressed him profoundly and later Modigliani cast a spell which he could never overcome. As an amiable, helpful figure in the artist-quarter he is always mentioned in those reminiscences of Paris which constitute so important a part of the history of the spirit of our time. Gertrude Stein writes of him affectionately, and Walt Kuhn has acknowledged his assistance in the preparation of the Armory show. In Maurer's own work the French influence had a curiously demoralizing effect. He went too far for his American friends but never far enough for his own satisfaction. His accomplishment cannot be properly estimated until the collections of several enthusiasts, particularly Messrs. Weyhe, Walker and Zigrosser, have been exhibited in their entirety. Certainly, out of his uneasy experiment, came now and then an odd first-rate picture. The self-portrait of 1926 reveals extraordinarily the excitement and sadness of a life which ended in suicide (page 77).

PROFESSIONAL PORTRAITISTS

Portraiture dates back to the dawn of civilization; indeed it can be traced further still, into shadowy, primitive time. But in the sense in which it is usually considered now—a more or less formal representation by a kind of artist who has made a specialty of it, to increase the sitter's self-esteem and semipublic prestige, or to satisfy the sentiment of his friends and relations—it does not rest upon as constant or as great a tradition down through the ages as one might suppose. Most of the masterpieces which our present academicians and professionals exalt as their ideal, which they emulate to the best of their ability and constantly cite to put our modernists to shame, were the occasional work of freer and more versatile men than they. Titian, Raphael, El Greco, Rubens—and Rembrandt, too, in his old age—excelled at all kinds of pictorial composition, imaginative or intellectual work, and, when they accepted a commission, recognized no particular subservience in it, no obligation to deliver a very exact or flattering likeness. In spirit and in their customary attitude towards the portrait-sitter they seem far closer to the modern school than to the docile, rapid, celebrated portraitists of today.

SARGENT is, perhaps, the epitome of the professional in the good nineteenth-century tradition. The unevenness of his work suggests that he may not have had so much plain talent as other successful men, but his taste was impeccable and he would work on obstinately until he saw something fine, and knew when to stop. His best work, such as the double portrait of Mrs. and Miss Warren (page 36), will charm generations to come just as the masterpieces of the English school have done. But what is most admired today is a smaller, sketchier type of likeness painted rather in the style of watercolor than oil paint, as a rule to please himself or some close friend.

BOLDINI stands higher than he did a few years ago, perhaps higher than Sargent. The virtue most apparent in his canvases is enthusiasm, especially with respect to female loveliness, which he portrayed in the height of the fashion of the time, so that his technique seemed to go out of style along with this apparel. Meanwhile, socialist idealism had begun to affect the general taste in art a little, and his exaltation of a plutocratic or parasitic society lost some of its charm. The work he did when he came to America, where he did not enjoy himself, seems a little hasty. But certain likenesses of young American womanhood represent our ideal of that era exquisitely. Miss Edith Blair (page 35) might be the heroine of a Henry James novel.

Every painter who has a flair for likeness and rapidity of execution must experience a moment of temptation to turn to this profitable specialty and to give up all else. The usual effect upon his painting is deplorable, and the more honestly he has worked in the modern way, depending upon inspiration and even improvisation, the worse it will be for him. The academic artist has at least an habitual, manual dexterity, and certain rules and devices. The modern, if he plays this dangerous game of portraiture for a fee, often settles into a slight, slick, deceitful technique, and a trademarked pulchritude, with no further development of either his sensibility or pictorial form.

VAN DONGEN in a large part of his career, and Derain, too, in recent years, have given us examples of this. In the heroic early days of modernism, suddenly, with some sense of inferiority, DERAIN destroyed most of the work he had done under Matisse's influence, about five years' work, and began his art over again, somewhat closer to Picasso for a while. From that point on the modern story has been enlivened by various proofs of his brilliant capability and by odd indications of his character, probably an unhappy character. Any artist who has enjoyed an exaggerated popularity, especially in a new style or styles, is subject to sudden reverses; certainly Derain has been.

He was never unpleasant or tragic in his modernity. He was a quick worker, so that there was plenty for the dealers to handle; and his fame grew almost as great as Matisse's or Picasso's. But early in the 'thirties, in serious circles of art, it began to be felt that he had become a cynical practitioner of hasty likenesses of pretty women

to almost as regrettable an extent as Van Dongen. The gifted young Polish-Parisian BALTHUS, whom he influenced, seems to have influenced him in turn, in any case stimulated him, beneficially. And so, just before the present war, his mercurial talent took a new direction, and he then painted a number of portraits which have an amiable aspect, well composed, in pleasing light color (page 101).

Those who think ill of Derain will be especially impressed by the contrast between the slight, grave self-portrait of his youth and Balthus' portrait of him in 1938, though probably the latter was done in friendly spirit (page 100). Here we see another of the functions of portraiture, rare because very few sitters will endure it; merciless annotations of character and the wear and tear of time; and, for a young man, Balthus is very good at it. Even the Wadsworth Atheneum's handsome picture of his wife is severe and full of anxious implication. For some time it has been apparent that, if he chose, he could have a great career of portraiture in a new grand manner; but of course the war has thrown all such things into obscurity.

Balthus' portrait of Miro (facing page 102) shows his talent in its best temper: simple and sober, with undertones, in this case affectionate. Putting it beside Miro's self-portrait (page 102) enables us to see the likeness in the great tangle of spidery lines and starry shapes of the latter. Some years ago MIRO used to do portraits of himself and of others in a way that might be called Spanish factualism; but now his subject matter is almost always unreal or at least remote. It is interesting to consider him for a moment, in passing, among the professional portraitists, for he is their exact antithesis.

For centuries Great Britain has been a great place for portraiture, especially in the formal manner, involving only a sedate, established kind of artistry. In his account of the great exhibition of British art at Burlington House in 1934, Roger Fry speaks of "the ominous preponderance of the portrait over all other kinds of picture"—and it still is so. The Royal Academy has kept more prestige than the corresponding institutions in other countries, and in its crowded annual exhibitions the portraits are the most popular feature. Thus a national interest in a repetitious type of artistic production has been maintained. Some years ago Wyndham Lewis' portrait of T. S. Eliot—of which we have the first version (page 92)—was rejected by the Academy, whereupon Augustus John resigned in protest. Lewis himself called it a "crushing and discouraging symbol of malignant and arrogant mediocrity." No doubt the harsh words were partly inspired by his personal disappointment, but we understand that good British artists of the younger generation all agree that the average of their portraiture today is not high. But there are the exceptions—Lewis and Henry Lamb and Coldstream and others—and celebrated portraitists whose careers on the whole are not exceptional in the least, also do some fine things now and then.

The Irishman, Sir William ORPEN, is a case in point. His industriousness, his alertness of mind and gusto—not unlike Boldini's but more concerned with manly character and career, less responsive to the beauty of women—resulted in an astonishingly long list of portraits of the great, especially financiers, statesmen and soldiers. Now that their time has passed, this worldly greatness has somewhat obscured the perspicacity about mere human nature and the honesty and even delicacy of technique which impress us in the portrait of Roland F. Knoedler (page 83). It is worth noting that this excellent work was not done in the usual professional circumstances, with fixed sittings and a deadline, for a fee, but just as any painter might paint one of his intimates or a member of his own family. Sir William and the distinguished art-dealer were lifelong associates, on very good terms. When he felt like painting he would inquire if his friend felt like posing; and so it went, little by little until it was completed, a labor of love.

Wherein we see once more, at its simplest, the true moral of the story of portraiture. Even the professional does his best work when his skill is supplemented by real familiarity and feeling, when his discipline and his objectivity are relaxed.

The unevenness of the work of Augustus JOHN. seems to derive rather from his character than from his career. One might say, using the words loosely, that he is a better artist than painter, which could not be said of Orpen. There is something unspoiled, but also undeveloped, about John's talent. Now he is an aging man, but one still thinks of him as a youthful genius. He has a decided originality of mind and a warm inspiration, but he seems never to have perfected his method of painting. It is not lack of energy or weakness of will—sometimes he requires a fantastic number of sittings—but as he works on doggedly, it is always towards an increasing dramatization of the first impression, a merely stronger statement, never towards finality of composition or refinement of style.

As a draughtsman John is in the first rank or very near it, as vigorous as a cartoonist, in the sketch of Lawrence of Arabia (page 74); as felicitous as the old masters, delicate in touch and sharp of eye, in the drawing of James Joyce. In his most famous large canvases—the portrait of the Marchesa Casati (page 75) and numerous, unforgettable likenesses of men, Joseph Widener, Gerald Massey, Gustav Stresemann— his feeling about human nature seems ruthless or malicious, his dramatic sense making the most of what he sees. Last year he was asked to paint the Queen of England, which he did, and then was given the Order of Merit. We have alluded to shortcomings of British taste in the matter of formal portraiture. But counting on the fingers of one hand the distinguished artists who have ever been asked to paint statesmen or statesmen's wives in our country, we realize one of our own shortcomings. We wish that the royal British example might be followed in Washington.

Formal portraiture has not flourished in the United States of late as richly as it has abroad; and much of the work here has been done by visiting foreign artists. With such able men as Speicher, Brackman and Philip on the national scene, one is inclined to attribute this to an un-American snobbery about things foreign. Many people have forgotten the lesson of the Eight, or never learned it. Speicher's portrait of Miss Cornell (page 91), Carroll's of Mrs. Ford, Brook's of Miss Hepburn, Brackman's of Bartlett Arkell, Schnakenberg's of Gerald McCann, should suit the requirements of the most captious friend or admirer.

Sometimes there is a lack of ardor, gusto, brio in American work of this kind, which may derive from something in the artist's own point of view about it. The good American creator is not often cynical like Boldini or Van Dongen, nor does he willingly resign himself to a lifetime of hard work and compliance in the worldly scheme of things as Sargent did. He keeps, as a rule, the idealism of his youth about art, and he may afterward be haunted by a sense of undeveloped powers in himself.

Alexander BROOK once wrote that "portrait commissions have ever been the bane of the artist's existence, in fact so much so that ordinarily he would rather do any form of manual labor than to accept the pesky sitter."* Many contemporary artists would agree with this, and those who do certainly should undertake a minimum of work to order. Any career begun with a prejudice so unhappy must end in some inhibition of talent. An artist can, of course, learn to do very well in a given convention, but if his heart is not in it something will be lacking. Brook, for example, has an obvious talent for clever, dignified, large portraiture, but he has done well to keep to small intimate pictures and portraits of friends like George Biddle (page 96) in which his sharp sensuous spirit appears without constraint. Carroll, too, excels in

* Creative Art, April, 1929.

delicate, sketchy likenesses of his beautiful wife, and of Dr. Valentiner's daughter and others.

THE POETICAL TRADITION

To turn from the successors of Sargent to Ensor, Rousseau, and our contemporaries akin to them, is a difficult transition. But the meaning of modern art often appears in such antitheses, and certainly the question of portraiture finally depends upon whether one prefers this extreme or that. Another great matter of preference sets the poetical or fantastic painters apart from the rest of the modern movement.

Perhaps in strict criticism one should never use the terminology of one art to describe another, but the subject of esthetics always needs to be simplified, especially in new manifestations. Those moderns whose inclination has been towards an abstract or purely formal development of painting—or to be more exact, their critics and interpreters—have borrowed vocabulary from architecture and music; and in the same way, as a convenience and a short cut, with reservations, the opposite type of artist can be loosely described in terms of literature.

The poetical moderns differ from the rest in this especially: they seem to have a greater concern with originalities of theme than with originalities of treatment, and there is always some unreality in their subject matter. Their world is a dream world. Naturally this extremely imaginative art is apt to be solitary and idiosyncratic. It does not lend itself well to the propounding of theory or to grouping in schools or movements, so it may be considered as it comes, personality after personality.

ENSOR is a great figure in this way. He is not well represented in American collections, but there eventually will be a wide interest in his personality and original style. His portraits are all intimate and all strange. Perhaps the finest is of his mother on her deathbed, with a still life of medicine bottles in front of her. Mr. Sam Salz owns a charming self-portrait inscribed, "Severe image of myself lit by moons," which shows him in old age, a gay, bright-eyed, bearded creature, and there are a couple of new moons up in one corner.

No one knows exactly how sane ROUSSEAU was, that is to say, how much objectivity or critical sense he maintained throughout his lonely creative life. Sometimes he daubed like a child, sometimes he composed immense difficult canvases with a magnificence and grace worthy of Uccello, and if he recognized the ups and downs of his talent himself he never admitted it. He did a number of portraits of himself and of both his wives. He painted Jarry and Pierre Loti and Joseph Brummer (page 57). He painted Apollinaire with Marie Laurencin beside him as his muse, measuring their faces again and again in order to get the likenesses exactly right. His gentle, heroic example has shed a kind of benediction upon modern art. Without it, for one thing, many men of our day would have had to work under the imputation of madness or foolishness. Those who have seen the masterpieces of this man, who was a figure of fun to most of those who knew him, may well hesitate to mock or despise any artist for his strangeness.

REDON is another admired example of the fantastic spirit and, especially in his lithographs, his style is closer to the twentieth-century fashion than Rousseau's. These dark little conceptions are not at all childlike; everything is in earnest, not so much make-believe as hallucination. His portraits, too, seem painted in a dream, but a harmless dream: heads coifed in antique style, or half-apparent in mist or surrounded by unbotanical flowers. He wrote intelligently, though not clearly, about his art, explaining that certain faces were the reality in the midst of his imagination, and the rest kaleidoscopic. The charming figure in Mr. Lewisohn's pastel appears to be Mme. Redon (page 41). It is her face also which peers forward in the Museum of Modern Art's "Silence," with one finger lifted to her lips. A number of the imaginative painters have been haunted for years like this by a beloved image, and therefore have made even of their fantasies a type of portraiture.

Then there is CHIRICO, the painter of empty cities and strange objects, a baffling figure in the story of modern art. Although an Italian he studied art at the Royal Academy in Munich. His early self-portrait with the motto in Latin—"What shall I love unless it be the enigma?"—shows an unusual mingling of the traditions of Germany and Italy (page 58). It is reminiscent of both Bellini and Böcklin. He painted his own likeness again and again, excitably, with a more and more forced air of genius.

His most important portrait is that of his father entitled "The Child's Brain" (page 59). It is a memory portrait, Chirico the elder having died nine years before, but evidently childish love and fear brought the serene, stout figure with naked torso to his mind more vividly and terribly than any living model. Chirico's talent has now changed so that his early admirers cannot recognize it, a mystery for the critics, to match the intimate mystery of "The Child's Brain." He still paints portraits in a prosaic, even academic fashion; his pretty wife among others, with waved hair and painted fingernails, in a gilt and brocade chair.

The other fantastic painter of that generation, CHAGALL, is a Russian, resident for a large part of his life in Paris, now resident here. The fantasy in his case derives from Hebrew poetry and custom, and from the folk art of his native land. It is a pleasant dream, not a nightmare. He keeps thinking of himself and beautiful Mme. Chagall as important immortal figures in theatrical scenes: himself, for example, borne pickaback by her with his characteristic bouquet of flowers, sky-high (page 65). In a plainer and more traditional Hebraic style, he has painted certain rabbis; the Art Institute's portrait of the Rabbi of Vitebsk is a superb work (page 64).

DUCHAMP'S career has been stranger than his art. Everyone seems persuaded of the genius of his youth; no one knows why he has steadfastly refused or neglected to paint for many years. His portraiture is almost unknown. To judge by Mr. Arensberg's handsome canvases (pages 60 and 61), perhaps he should not be considered in this fantastic lineage at all, but rather among Cézanne's followers. From the strong design of "The Sonata," the odd refraction of the light in angles away from the four figures in it, one supposes that he might have devised an art of abstract representation as original as Picasso's cubist portraits if he had wanted to. Strangely lacking in ambition, disrespectful of most things, true to nothing except his seemingly perfect intelligence, he has preferred not to develop his inspirations. In his young manhood he lived in the United States for a number of years, and now he is back here, where he may be expected to exercise an influence upon young artists even if he will not, or cannot, set them a good example. He may be called a surrealist, by temperament if not in the method of his art, and lately he has collaborated with the present organized group.

DALI, who to the general public personifies surrealism (page 105), is no longer acceptable to the group. In any case there is nothing much in the way of problematical esthetics in his portraiture: a factual representation of the sitter, sometimes in oppressive physical detail, with slight objects of psychological significance placed roundabout, as in days gone by portrait painters introduced still life à la mode.

The Museum of Modern Art's double portrait is one of the best known and most pleasing of a number of likenesses of Mme. Dali. He admires Meissonier and is second only to Chirico in admiration of Böcklin. Whether or not he has felt any other German influence—that of Dix, for example, to which some of the younger Americans have responded—is hard to tell. There has been a return everywhere lately to a certain classic virtuosity; one of those vague effects of the *Zeitgeist* which, in the long run, have been stronger in modern art than organized changes of style. The art historian has hastened to trace the latter,

and presently the general historian may make sense of the entire spirit, relating it to the rest of our culture and our general fate.

Among the surrealists in good standing (1942), Max ERNST and Leonora CARRINGTON both have a gift of resemblance and notable invention to display their sense of the character of the sitter. They may have influenced each other's surrealism a little, but the portraits of her by them show the differentiation of their talent very well (page 122). She has a limited but pathetic inspiration like that of a fairy tale; whereas his figures are all set in a rich, operatic investiture. Some years ago he often worked in photomontage; a number of the surrealists and others have condescended to this semi-artistic device. GROSZ used it in the early 'twenties in a spirit of political and sociological as well as esthetic rebellion (page 71). Max Ernst's way was a rather frivolous borrowing of his principal imagery from the common or the traditional stock, and the wit of it lay in certain embellishments or desecrations. His recent pictures have a real virtuosity in which a new vein of his imagination appears.

The latest of the surrealists to command great respect is the Belgian, Paul DELVAUX. His compositions might be scenes in a poetical drama. Inside or outside stylized buildings, or in imaginary gardens, appear likenesses of the same beautiful girl, and we are told that this is recognizably a tribute to his wife (page 123).

TCHELITCHEW is one of those who stoutly deny any connection or sympathy with surrealism, whom the surrealists scarcely admire, but whom the public still persistently calls by that name. In the correct parlance he is a neo-romantic, but the slightest comparison with the work of others who are so entitled suggests that this, too, is inadequate or inaccurate.

The art of Tchelitchew cannot be characterized briefly because it is many-sided and, furthermore, contains considerable mystery. The origins of his style and the importance of his pictures have been finely analyzed by James Thrall Soby in a recent publication of the Museum of Modern Art. He does not work canvas by canvas, nor does he repeat; it is a lifework, one of those cases in which, by the power of art, a reasonable order and philosophy are imposed upon a genuine anarchy of emotion. But he is worldly and in his numerous portraits there is not an excessive self-expression. The conventionality and timidity which portrait commissions induce in many artists seem never to affect him, because of his spontaneity and strength of ego. It is his way to romanticize the appearance and aggrandize the character of all his subjects; whether this may be said to be flattery or not depends on the point of view. The portraits of Joella Lloyd and of Lincoln Kirstein (pages 103 and 118) are characteristic examples. For a decade or more he has been famous as a draughtsman. The great display of this gift is in his portraits in silverpoint, that peculiar old medium which does not permit the least erasure.

BÉRARD is a master of decorative painting. Within the limits of his energy and of the modesty or parsimony of our way of habitation, he is the contemporary Tiepolo. Not many of his portraits have been brought to this country; they seem less strong and less finished than his romantic compositions. The double self-portrait entitled "On the Beach" is exceptional, with a representation of the faces as distinct as David or Courbet, the pose and the scene strangely touching (page 104). The portraits of BERMAN are attractive and fanciful, with what appears to be a deliberate sacrifice of resemblance for the sake of personification. In a series of portraits of the cinematographic actress, Miss Munson, he has portrayed her in various décors as a great muse (page 132).

The painters who are called primitives—that is, those who most conspicuously lack that diversity of skill which we find in a Picasso or a Tchelitchew —have brought a great honor to the modern movement. There is nothing disparaging in the word now; but there has been inconsistency in the general use of it. One is tempted to apply it to Miss STETTHEIMER, but as she is an artist of great culture it is hard to explain exactly why. Perhaps she pretends to be simple, or encourages a reputation of slight eccentricity in order to keep out of the critical limelight and the debating of esthetics. Her art has been a private commemoration of the enjoyments of a lifetime in the circle of her family and friends. From picture to picture she has continued her account of things, like an album or a diary. To criticize or catalog it properly would require a knowledge and iconography of almost all the artistic side of New York life in the last three decades. In a sense it is all portraiture. As a rule in her individual portraits she places the sitter in a formal, central posture, filling the background with little episodes in which he appears again in characteristic activity, as in representations of the saints in the art of the cinquecento. Sometimes she adopts a more abstract design, as in the portrait of Marcel Duchamp. Sometimes she shows a mild, modest expressionism as in the portrait of her sister with the Christmas tree (page 80). Perhaps it is incorrect to call this a poetical art; it is rather like a novel and in a way, as Marsden Hartley has observed in one of his subtle essays, it makes one think of Marcel Proust.

Marsden HARTLEY is the best known and the eldest of the very romantic, that is, unrealistic, American painters, but he bears no similarity to the fantastic school of Europe and his present subject matter is what is sometimes called Americana. He always showed a strongly American temperament. In 1928 he wrote that in his youth he had followed a principle of Blake's: "Put off intellect and put on imagination; the imagination is the man." He no longer believed in imagination; his faith for the sake of his art had turned to intellectual clarity. "I have come to the conclusion that it is better to have two colors in right relation to each other than to have a vast confusion of emotional exuberance or poetical revelation . . . I had rather be intellectually right than emotionally exuberant, and I could say this in any other aspect of my personal experience."* Although written in strong New England style, with no airs or graces except those of conviction, the sense of this remarkable statement was not so dogmatic or final as it seemed. He went on to specify that the intellectuality in question had reference to the knowledge of how to paint: science of color, mastery of pictorial construction, for which he was happy to sacrifice for a time his self-expression. Lately the lyricism has come back to his work, fortified and warmer than ever. "I do not care for portraits," he has said, "outside of Memling and one or two others, I never saw a portrait by anyone that made me feel one could trust it. I only believe in likeness, and there is a difference, as a likeness can be an aspect and the flat portrait cannot." His extraordinary image of Albert P. Ryder, which contrasts so strangely with the portraits by Weir and Miller, is a memory portrait: the old mystic painter as Hartley had seen him now and then in the last years of his life, always by night. "Adelard the Drowned" is also a remembered image (page 115) and illustrates most clearly that power of tenderness and tragic sense which the spontaneous technique of his first period could never have conveyed.

TWO KINDS OF REALISM

Most American portraiture today is realism, but two distinct ways of painting come under this heading: a minute and finished and sometimes literal rendering on the one hand and, on the other, a style which descends from impressionism and from Sargent and the Eight. The precise method may be said to represent a certain departure from the leadership of France in modern art.

The painters of the Netherlands and Germany seem never to have had as much architectural sense or feeling for decorative pattern as the

* Marsden Hartley, "Art—And the Personal Life," Creative Art, Vol. II, No. VI, xxxi.

Italian and the French. On the other hand they have often taken a more intent and humble interest in the reality of their subject matter. In Germany, perhaps because of the glory of Holbein and Dürer, this tradition has been maintained through the nineteenth century to date as if it were a national heritage. The Swiss shared in it; even HODLER occasionally exemplifies it (page 58), although his monumental compositions have had greater acclaim, and some German critics, and at least one American authority, have found some resemblance to Cézanne in them.

In twentieth-century Germany DIX is or was the most notable exponent of the Germanic realism. He began in an almost academic way as we see in his self-portrait with the carnation (page 70). During the war, in the depressive spirit from which Germans suffer at times, there developed within his classic mentality a most modern virulence, misanthropic or at all events anti-bourgeois. As a leader of the neo-objective school, Neue Sachlichkeit, he had success and almost popularity, while Germany's modernism lasted. Now it is reported that the new regime has restricted him to painting landscape. His formal portrait of Fraülein Berber must be one of the most disagreeable pictures in the world. The Museum of Modern Art's portrait of Dr. Meyer-Hermann shows his more admiring or at least respectful mood (page 70).

Meanwhile a number of artists in other countries had begun to take a view of art which bore some relation to Neue Sachlichkeit, whether by direct influence or merely in the spirit of the time. The veracity of the detail in surrealism, irrespective of the truth of the picture as a whole, has already been mentioned. A change of orientation began in the United States also, and certain of our young men of talent went to Germany instead of Paris. Our present school of minutely realistic painters, while not numerous, is of considerable interest for the future.

There is something equivocal in extremely exact realism; there always has been. The feeling in it, whether it is love or hate, respect or spite, is pinned down so closely to the factual detail that one can scarcely be sure of it. One is troubled by this a little in the work of the late Grant WOOD. His memorable "American Gothic" is emphatic in one way but uncertain in another (page 99). Is it a harsh lampoon, or is it a manner of praise of the important representative types of American portrayed in it? He himself said, "I admit the fanaticism and false taste of the characters in 'American Gothic,' but to me they are basically good and solid people." His later portraits show his good nature; a very wholesome but not very vigorous humanity. The chief weakness of his work is the delicacy of his execution, the faint color lying rather dustily upon the careful form. When one has seen it in black-and-white reproduction, one is often disappointed by the original.

SHEELER is a more earnest, subtle artist than Wood was. A wonderfully faithful portraiture might be expected of him; he has not often cared to undertake it. BLUME and ATHERTON have both worked in a way of mixed abstraction and surrealism, but one feels that a more objective art may suit them better in the end, and they have shown a gift for portraiture.

It is doubtful whether ALBRIGHT owes much to the Germans or to any example or teaching. His character and his interests would have been exceptional in any country and era. Leisurely and aristocratic in disposition, he takes infinite pains with his pictures until they become almost frightening in their precision (page 124). Perhaps no one since Grünewald has so intently rendered the very grain of human skin, the perishable matter in which the soul is enveloped, and also the apathy of the soul, not able to shine through the flesh and bone. If he had not kept to his Middle West, in most of his subject matter as well as in residence, he might also have been called a surrealist.

CADMUS, who explicitly admires Dix, is the best-known precise painter of the younger generation. He draws well. His early work was bitterly humor-

ous in style though without a very distinct satiric point or program. He is an able portrait painter, and as he has painted only friends his portraiture has all been benign. Perhaps the bitterness is going out of his imagination. He enjoys a certain complexity of composition, and therefore occasionally paints conversation pieces. His portrait of a farmer and his wife with their fine livestock (page 130) makes a striking contrast with "American Gothic."

All these Americans who paint with careful detail have one other thing in common, and apparently it is in the American tradition, for we find it in amateur and provincial painting all the way back to Colonial times, and in the work of Audubon, and in the best of Homer and Eakins. It is a certain liking for neat and distinct form somewhat silhouetted in a rather vacuous bright space. In our country even the bad weather is brilliant, and the light is absolute, clean and in a way merciless; and perhaps it is not fanciful to think that this may have affected our pictorial style in many cases.

There is also a moral implication in our new realism; something akin to that scruple and self-conscious orderliness in life which, sometimes carelessly, we call puritanism. It is not really new, and it lies deeper than sophistication; a point upon which the spirit of our primitive or self-taught painters is very revealing. The greatest of them, John KANE, wrote in his autobiography: "I take pains with my work. One thing that I cannot abide is sloppy work in any form. I think a painting has a right to be as exact as any joist or a mold or any other part of building construction. I think the artist owes it to the people to make his painting as right and sound as he can make it."*

This seems a natural, noble principle, and it might serve as a text for the intolerance which some young artists now feel towards certain of their more celebrated elders in this country. But if they will take it as their text, they have a long and

* *Sky Hooks: The Autobiography of John Kane*, 1938, page 172.

26

difficult road in art, especially in portrait painting, where time usually presses, and the presence and mood of the sitter are apt to increase whatever self-consciousness the painter may suffer from. For that obligation of good workmanship, so simple in the mind of the carpenter-painter Kane, entails for sophisticated realists—men like Blume, Cadmus, French, Guglielmi, Atherton, Rain—an incessant investigation and exercise of the entire range of pictorial capability, including a better thought and mastery of the formal aspect of construction than most of them have shown so far. Then, too, there is the risk of lack of imagination. This is one of the regular risks of puritanism, in art as in ethics: it serves as a great stimulant during one's education and in hardship, but when the goal comes in sight it sometimes lapses into complacency or a kind of immobility of mind. If their hard work and conscience does not inhibit the imagination, they may change the aspect of our modern art considerably.

Of course the opposite principle is still held by the majority. In BIDDLE'S autobiography there is this sentence: "All of us are sometimes driven by lack of public understanding, by some middle-class morality, by our inhibition or cowardice, to conceive of art as cabinet-work, not duly completed until it has been sandpapered or varnished."*

This is not a perfectly clear statement; it does, however, appear to give the lie direct to John Kane, oddly enough with the very analogy that came naturally to him. It implies a strange resentment of the ethical obligation to do one's best, hinting at some instinctive dislike of craftsmanship, a manner of puritanism in reverse. Biddle's portrait of Mrs. Zorach (page 97) suggests no such drastic carelessness, but there are a great many successful painters who not only suggest but exemplify and personify it. In portraiture, coarseness or hastiness of execution is especially troubling, and bravery of color, knack of likeness, show of strength, never quite make up for it.

* George Biddle: *An American Artist's Story*, page 227.

At its best, informal realism—that is, the quicker, rougher style derived from the nineteenth-century French masters and from the Eight in this country—can be as fine as the new realism, or finer. SOYER and HIRSCH paint portraits in the free style (pages 111 and 131), showing very little influence of the modern school of Paris, and certainly not a trace of German neo-objectivity. They are gifted, and they need no particular warning unless it be against that success and opportunity to undertake too much work which they are certain to have before long.

GROPPER is best known for his genre painting, which has a decided social significance as a rule. His portraits, often not so entitled, are lively and very true to type. Ben SHAHN, so strange in some of his figure pictures as to suggest mysticism, has gone further than Gropper in political aggressiveness, oddly enough by means of a jeering or a pathetic portraiture (page 94).

Three very distinguished American painters in the established, more or less French tradition, are Walt Kuhn, Watkins and Poor. Walt KUHN has had a leading role in our art on the progressive side for many years, ever since the Armory Exhibition. He probably could have been, if he had chosen to be, our foremost portrait painter. As it is, he is the chief of those who prefer the generalized portrayal of types of humanity to the specific characterization of the model before him, who generally have been excluded from the present selection; and recognizing the power or the charm of his various figure-pictures, one could scarcely complain of his preference. The distinction between true portraiture and figure-painting, as noted in an early paragraph of this text, is impossible to make exactly; the admirable "Man from Eden" (page 95) is said to be a good likeness.

The work of WATKINS is more elegant than that of either Kuhn or Poor, with exquisite nuances of color and a seemingly casual linear technique which nevertheless defines its form very clearly.

It is rather French in spirit, but it would be hard to cite anything of recent date in France with this fine balance of dignity and wit. The informal portrait of the twins and the poodle has charm in the specific pictorial sense as well as in subject and sentiment (color plate facing page 116). Sensitive to various types of sitter, in his portraits of men his style changes unaffectedly, as if by instinct, and with a certain abruptness of outline and angularity of gesture gives a particular effect of intelligence and strength (page 116).

There is no such grace and easiness in the work of POOR. His technique has a certain rugged appearance, and is sometimes painstaking, but with a bold disposition of compact forms within the space of the canvas. At his best he has fine color, subdued and unified, clothing the form without distracting attention from it. "The Chess Game" is typical of his most personal vein, and the close fitting together of the two figures and the mysterious implication of the fine hand poised over the definite rectangle of the chessboard are most imaginative (page 107).

LATIN AMERICANS

Owing to difficulties of communication and transportation arising from the war, it has been impossible to survey with justice the field of portraiture in Latin America. The art of Mexico, however, is fairly well understood in the United States, where it has had great influence. Most of the great Mexican artists believed in the revolution and assisted in it by painting murals which inculcated in their people the conviction and emotion of the great political and economic changes which were taking place. These murals constitute one of the real glories of modern art, and in them there is to be found a great deal of portraiture of the various leaders. But one must go there to appreciate them. RIVERA'S large painting of Guadalupe Marín (page 127), the model for some of the principal figures in his heroic decorations, shows the style of his monumental portraiture.

OROZCO has painted a number of portraits, of which the recent one of Sra. Gurza is especially strong and grave, with an expression of idealistic self-consciousness (page 126). Like certain expressionists in this as in some other respects, he has painted himself many times; the self-portrait belonging to the Museum of Modern Art is the boldest in technique and a fine likeness (page 125).

The fiery SIQUEIROS has done unconventional easel portraits, and in the romantic vein they are extraordinary. His likeness of María Asúnsolo as a child, shown in the Museum's exhibition, "Twenty Centuries of Mexican Art," is one of the most admired, and a powerful, though fractional, self-portrait is included here (page 125).

Frida KAHLO portrays herself again and again, but in a surrealist rather than expressionist spirit (page 127). MONTENEGRO is a worldly but poetical artist who has painted the Vice-President of the United States, and, recently, George Hoyningen-Huene. O'GORMAN, who did the murals at the Central Airport in Mexico City, is a brilliant practitioner of minute realism.

Lately Mexico City has become more cosmopolitan, and the fanatic political days appear to be over. Therefore many younger men such as GALVAN and SORIANO have been developing a more eclectic, polished manner (page 126). One almost regrets this, because the pictorial culture of Europe now seems less promising for them than their own great national tradition. MEZA is a very young painter of great interest, precisely because he is faithful to the deep, truly Mexican inspiration (page 128).

SCULPTORS

The course of modern portrait sculpture has been less troubled and less disputed than that of painting. Brancusi and Henri Laurens, Lipchitz and Zadkine, Calder and Dlugosz have made considerable innovations, but rarely in portraiture.

The greatest single influence in modern portrait sculpture has been RODIN (page 37). Although his extraordinary productivity kept up until 1916, his fluent technique seems closer to impressionism than to our present sense of the beauties of bronze and marble. His portraiture is not very poetical. There is often an excessive detail, both of character and of loveliness.

But underneath the arresting, blurring surface, sculptors have never failed to note a certain fidelity to the solid and truthful form. Rodin was an instinctive and egocentric, rather than an intelligent, man. In the endless record of his opinion which his pupils and admirers kept there is nothing very notable, and yet he must have been a great teacher. Despiau worked in his studio and Brancusi was his pupil for a while, and they have been the two most influential masters of the last two decades, conveying something of his spirit. Even LIPCHITZ has expressed a specific admiration of him,* and in recent years he, and ZADKINE as well (pages 67, 114 and 121), have returned occasionally to a simple representational technique which may owe something to his powerful although careless example.

MAILLOL, who seems more like a Greek than any other modern man (perhaps a Theocritan, that is, a Sicilian Greek), has bent his energies so entirely to a pursuit of ideal beauty in sculpture that he has not found time for portraiture. He has stated his feeling about it in the simplest terms:

"I do not do portraits. I make heads in which I try to give an impression of the whole. I am tempted by the head when I can find an architecture in it . . . I did not wish to undertake a bust of Mme. de Noailles because Rodin did it, and his is very beautiful (page 37). I am not the right man to make heads of well-known people."

How superbly he could do it, if he chose, is shown by his affectionate likeness of Renoir (page 39). The aged painter sat to him seven days, patiently, without painting. On the last day the clay collapsed in a heap on the floor. The tears

* Cahiers d'Art, No. 5, 1930, p. 263.

came to Renoir's eyes. Touched by this, Maillol took heart and produced this noble bust at one sitting. His charming head of Cézanne's daughter-in-law, Renée Rivière, also shows the great aptitude which he has not cared to practice.

Even for his goddesses he has always found models so extraordinarily alike, and of a type so close to the perfection in his mind, that one is tempted to consider some of his monumental works, too, as a kind of portraiture. The source of a concept of impersonal beauty such as Maillol's is doubtless individual appearance, and shows us the connection between the portrait and the more purely imaginative types of art. The impersonal artist seeks corroboration in reality, to renew or to verify his imagination.

The style of DESPIAU (pages 108 and 109) is a kind of modernization of Rodin. It is as if by working down through the top layer of one of Rodin's brilliant busts we discovered the clear, convincing shape, rotund and truly constructed. From the particular standpoint of portraiture, in astuteness of characterization and suggestion of the way of life of the sitter, something is lost. When it is most beautiful it conforms to a concept of French womanhood, serene and forceful and enigmatic. There is, perhaps, too marked a kinship between one face and another. Apparently Despiau cares more for this general beauty than for any particular reality, either physiological or psychological. But he is probably the most sought-after sculptor of portraits in the world, and in the universal acceptance of his work, in spite of its austerity, we see how closely his ideal lies to our present sensibility.

The Rumanian BRANCUSI departed the farthest from the method of Rodin and from the Greek representational tradition. The point of departure—that is, Rodin's influence—is very obvious in an early bronze head of a little sickly-looking boy, but it is far more pathetic and direct than anything by the great Parisian. There is a drawing of another small child inscribed by Brancusi with these words: "Simplicity is not a proper objective in art, but you come to it in spite of yourself as you approach the real significance of things." No doubt he has arrived in the same way at his extremes of abstraction. But simplicity is not the whole story in his case. His imagination has also a fabulous, audacious, Oriental quality; it stops at nothing. The famous bust of Mlle. Pogany, which in its first version in veined marble so startled the innocent crowds at the Armory Exhibition in 1913, is perhaps even handsomer in gleaming bronze (page 68).

Jacob EPSTEIN is world-famous for one or two of his dramatic monuments, but perhaps his reputation with the elite is not so high as it deserves to be. His series of likenesses in bronze of famous figures—Joseph Conrad, Einstein (page 120), Shaw, Lord Fisher, Lady Gregory, John Dewey (page 93) and others—is a galaxy even more historic than Rodin's. In portraiture the fame of the subject certainly counts if the artist is able to convey it without vulgar emphasis. One of Professor Dewey's family remarked that Epstein had made him look like a Vermont horse-dealer, and the force of this portrait is less a matter of emphasis than acumen. One aspect of Epstein's talent is a kind of excitement, a complete absorption in the personality before him. He is over-expressive, as Rodin was, but more so, with no Parisian good taste to stop him. One might say that Epstein is a greater portraitist than artist. In other words, his reaction to the sitter is more important than his sensitivity to the medium he works in. It is a kind of journalism but in a sense of that word which cannot be disrespectfully intended; for it reports subject matter of real importance with simplicity, sometimes coarsely, but handsomely.

Generally speaking, the excellent American sculptors of our generation—Zorach, Noguchi and Baizerman, for example, and the Misses Scaravaglione, Harkavy and Gershoy—have been more influenced by the elder Parisian masters than by the one great American, Lachaise; which

seems odd, but may have been a sound inclination, to their artistic advantage on the whole. For LACHAISE had a singular genius, and his supreme technical accomplishment was all directed to a particular self-expression. It might have been impossible to learn much from his way of working without deriving some mannerism or insincerity of style from his exceedingly original spirit.

As the time passes we begin to feel that his famous monumental nudes may not be his masterpieces, after all. There is a certain overstatement in them, as if he did not know his own strength. But surely the marble bust of George L. K. Morris (page 86) is perfect, more controlled and finely finished than anything of the kind by Rodin or Despiau. Perhaps a dozen other portraits are first-rate, and so are the small bronze figures: the nude portrait of Lincoln Kirstein, and another nude with a tennis racket, which belongs to Mr. Morris.

"At twenty, in Paris," Lachaise wrote, "I met a young American person who immediately became the primary inspiration which awakened my vision and the leading influence that has directed my forces. Through my career as an artist, I refer to this person by the word, Woman."* He went on to say that after he came to America, "Woman as a vision sculptured began to move, vigorously, robustly, alert, lightly, radiating sex and soul. . . ." No doubt this is a tribute to his wife, and perhaps in this passage he was referring particularly to one of the first of his remarkable images of her, "Woman Walking" (page 86), which in any case it described very well. The unique thing about his art is its power to convey intense romantic emotion like this convincingly in simple, single figures, without any literary allusion or dramatic arrangement. His words are awkward and over-emphatic, but in the exquisitely finished bronze he expresses himself as if it were in perfect rhyme and meter, as one can imagine Shelley's doing if he had been a sculptor.

* Creative Art, August, 1928.

He has had great praise but he is still, relatively speaking, a neglected artist. Comparing one of his bronze heads, that of John Marin for example (page 87), with similar work by Epstein or Rodin, it is easy to see the truly sculptural style which constitutes his superiority. There is a lack of substantiality in Epstein, and in Rodin the basic shape is somewhat covered up with his impressionistic modelling; whereas in Lachaise—even in this example, where he has worked a little roughly to catch the likeness—the inner form and its outer envelope, the simple design and the polished surface of metal on which the eye rests, seem identical.

French by birth, Lachaise seems very American —luxurious in his handling of his medium, enthusiastic about the human body as well as the spirit, jovial and tender—and evidently he seemed American to himself at the end of his life. "For a time I remained in France lazily contemplating masterpieces of the past. Then in 1906 I left for America. *Wake up*, the interjection of a street-car conductor inducing me to act, should illustrate what I mean when I say that the New World is the most favorable place to develop a creative artist. . . ." This is a moving statement now, when so many artists have been obliged to come across the Atlantic, for North and South America were made by immigrants like Lachaise who were able to find the newness that they had anticipated.

ON COMMISSIONING PORTRAITS

The fact is that the very best portraiture cannot be simply commissioned. Mere money is not enough. The spirit of the artist has to be met halfway. If you want a really good portrait, the wisest course is to make friends with the artist. Previous to the work of art or concurrently with it there must be some mutuality of feeling and compatibility of mind. If it does not exist, it must somehow be established before inspiration can take its proper flight, before the sculptor's hand or the painter's

brush or the draughtsman's pen can function with unrestrained felicity and skill.

This explains why the larger proportion of the best portraits today commemorate a close personal connection of some sort that bridges the distance between one psyche and another in the enforced intimacy of the studio. Portraiture must be a kind of collaboration. Where there is disrespect, or conventional or pretended enthusiasm, nothing much of artistic value is likely to come of it. A really good portrait is a rare thing, and misunderstanding or neglect of the strict nature of the joint responsibility for it is one reason why it is rare.

But there are other types of trouble to which portraiture is subjected: prejudice, momentary shrinking from reality, and too little imagination, too late. In 1887 the Union League of Philadelphia commissioned Eakins to paint a portrait of the then President of the United States, Rutherford B. Hayes. It was midsummer, and Eakins moved his easel into the presidential office and painted him as he sat working at his desk in his shirt sleeves. This disappointed and shocked the Union League. They grudgingly paid the artist his fee but would never hang the portrait in their clubrooms, and eventually it was destroyed or lost. Fifteen years after Hayes' death Eakins was asked to re-paint him from memory. He did so, but could not finish it, and it is not a masterpiece.

John Rewald, in an important monograph on Seurat soon to be published, tells us upon Robert Rey's authority that in the original version of Seurat's "*La Poudreuse*," the portrait of Madeleine Knoblock in the Courtauld Collection, there was also a little self-portrait reflected in the mirror of the dressing table at which she sits powdering her face. One of his friends protested against this, saying that fun would be made of it, and Seurat, who never shrank from mockery on his own account, was apparently anxious to protect Mlle. Knoblock from it. He obliterated his face from the looking glass and substituted the bouquet of flowers as it is now. The consequence is that we do not know what this great artist looked like. No photographs of him have ever come to light, and the written descriptions of him do not agree. The friend in question lived to regret his destructive suggestion, but posterity, to whom Seurat will mean more and more as one of the great initiators of a future art, is bound to blame him for it, and those who take an interest in psychology may well wonder about his perhaps unconscious motivation.

Some years ago the brilliant Mexican painter, Siqueiros, painted a portrait of Hart Crane. A fortnight before that gifted American poet took his own life he brought out the canvas to show it to some friends, flew into a rage against it and slashed it to bits, perhaps a rehearsal of that death upon which his erroneous energetic spirit was bent.

The obscure impulse of iconolatry and iconoclasm appears to be a profound trait of the human psyche. Throughout the world it has always been one of the tenets of primitive religion that the magic of a god or a man resides more or less in a likeness of him, and that, through one ritual or another, it is possible to partake of that magic, or on the other hand, by destroying the image, to negate what it stands for. Thus we may perhaps trace the origin and heredity of portraiture back to the childhood and childishness of the human race. And a little ancient superstition and piety sometimes cling to it in our minds without our recognizing them.

We mention this as a counsel of patience and sense of humor both to those who wish to have their portraits painted and to the artists who are willing to paint them. In this category of art far too many people of progressive taste, as well as born reactionaries, approach the artist with a strange alarm and uneasiness. They seem to feel that the least deviation from that image of themselves of which they find a corroboration in the mirror or in photography is an indignity and a disadvantage which may do harm in some psychological sense, in their own or others' estimation. Whereas departure from ordinary imagery, departure from reality itself, is essential to art.

The artist himself is often of two minds about portraiture and may assume one extreme attitude or another; an easy cynicism on the one hand, or unhappy puritanical refusal on the other. Sometimes artists who have a natural gift for it refuse it disdainfully.

The paucity of good art in the bulk of portrait painting today would not seem unreasonable if those who go to expensive professionals got the exact likenesses they have in mind. But, by their own account, as a rule they do not. It is a matter of confused psychology impinging or encroaching upon esthetics. It may be incorrigible or, perhaps, as in other cases of prejudice and inhibition, a little light shed on the problem as a whole, by comparisons and juxtapositions, may help to change our point of view.

As the reader examines the catalog at the end of this volume, he will find many important items which have not been mentioned in this brief survey, and ample proof that there is a great deal of fine contemporary portraiture. But, as we have said before, it is regrettable that so few of the great of our era have been painted by the artists who are most admired. One would like to commission a portrait of President Roosevelt by Franklin Watkins, of Vice-President Wallace by Marsden Hartley, of Einstein by Marc Chagall or Max Weber, or of Miss Garbo by Tchelitchew, for example.

But public greatness and immortality are not all. In that accumulation of the art of the ages which all the world treasures and which serves as a durable basis of our education and civilized faith, portraits of someone's grandmother, or wife, or husband, or child, count for almost as much as the iconography of the saints and geniuses and heroes. And this belief permits us, upon the evidence of the work listed here, to praise sincerely the achievement of living artists.

EAKINS: Miss Elizabeth L. Burton, 1906. Oil, 30 x 25". Minneapolis Institute of Arts, Minneapolis.

MAURER: The Black Parasol (Miss Gabrielle), 1901–03. Oil, 36 x 29". Buchholz Gallery, New York.

BOLDINI: Miss Edith Blair, 1902. Oil, 57 x 36". Collection Miss Edith Blair, Marseille, France.   **35**

SARGENT: Mrs. Fiske Warren and her Daughter, 1903. Oil, 60 x 40½". Collection Mrs. Warren
Lothrop, Cambridge, Massachusetts.

above: RODIN: Mme. X (Comtesse Mathieu de Noailles), c. 1907. Marble, 19½″ high. Metropolitan
   Museum of Art, New York.
below: RODIN: Thomas Fortune Ryan, c. 1910–11. Bronze, 23″ high. Metropolitan Museum of Art, New
   York.

above: RENOIR: Claude Renoir Painting, 1906. Oil, 21¼ x 17½". Collection Mr. and Mrs. Josiah
Titzell, Georgetown, Connecticut.

below: RENOIR: Coco (the artist's youngest son, Claude), 1905. Bronze, 10¾" high. Collection Miss
Mabel Choate, New York.

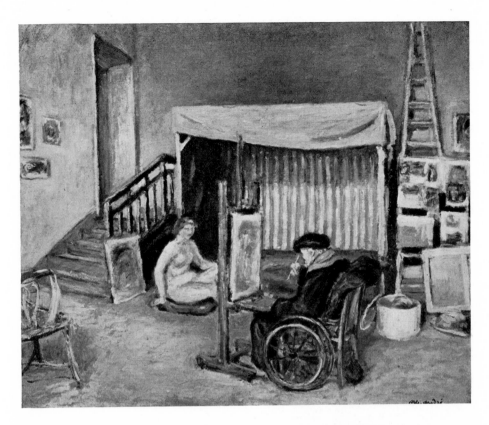

above: ANDRÉ: Renoir in his Studio, 1916. Oil, 19¾ x 24″. Durand-Ruel, New York.
below: MAILLOL: Auguste Renoir, 1907. Bronze, 15″ high. The Museum of Modern Art, New York.
Gift of Mrs. Cornelius J. Sullivan, in memory of Cornelius J. Sullivan.

VUILLARD: The Painter Ker-Xavier Roussel and his Daughter, c. 1900. Oil on cardboard, 23 x 21″. Collection André Weil, New York.

REDON: Dream Shadows. Pastel, 19½ x 25″. The Lewisohn Collection, New York.

RENOIR: Mother and Child (Frau Thurneyssen and her Daughter), 1910. Oil, 39⅜ x 31½". Albright
Art Gallery, Buffalo.

VUILLARD: Théodore Duret, 1912. Oil on wood, 37 x 29¼". Chester Dale Collection, New York.

BONNARD: The Checkered Dress (Mme. Pierre Bonnard), 1928. Oil, 30⅞ x 18⅝″. Collection Laurance S. Rockefeller, New York.

HENRI: The Masquerade Dress (Mrs. Robert Henri), 1911. Oil, 77 x 37". Collection Miss Violet Organ, New York.

SLOAN: Yeats at Petitpas (Van Wyck Brooks, John Butler Yeats, Alan Seegar, Mrs. John Sloan, Celestine Petitpas, Robert W. Sneddon, Anne Squire, John Sloan, Fred King and Mrs. Charles Johnston), 1910. Oil, 26 x 32". The Corcoran Gallery of Art, Washington, D. C.

GLACKENS: Family Group (Irene Dimock, Mrs. William J. Glackens, Ira Glackens, Mrs. D. H. Morgan),
1910. Oil, 72 x 84". Collection Mrs. William J. Glackens, New York.   47

above: LAURENCIN: Group of artists (Picasso, Fernande Olivier, Guillaume Apollinaire and the artist), 1908. Oil, 24¾ x 31⅛". Collection Miss Etta Cone, Baltimore.

below left: PICASSO: Fernande Olivier, 1905. Bronze, 14" high. Buchholz Gallery, New York.

below center: PICASSO: Woman's Head (Fernande Olivier), 1906. Charcoal drawing. Not in the exhibition.

below right: PICASSO: Woman's Head, 1909? Bronze, 16¼" high. The Museum of Modern Art, New York. Mrs. John D. Rockefeller, Jr. Purchase Fund.

PICASSO: Fernande , 1908. Oil, 24¼ x 16¾". Bignou Gallery, New York.

GRIS: Pablo Picasso, 1912. Oil, 36¼ x 28¾". Bignou Gallery, New York. Not in the exhibition.

above: PICASSO: Ambroise Vollard, 1910. Oil. Not in the exhibition.
below: BRASSAÏ: Ambroise Vollard, 1935. Photograph.

above: PICASSO: Gertrude Stein, 1906. Oil. Collection Miss Gertrude Stein, Paris. Not in the exhibition.

below: MAN RAY: Gertrude Stein, Photograph.

MATISSE: The Woman with a Hat (Mme. Henri-Matisse), 1905. Collection Mrs. Michael Stein, Palo Alto, California. Not in the exhibition.

MATISSE: Woman's Head (Jane Vaderin), c. 1908. Bronze, 12″ high. Collection Dr. and Mrs. Harry Bakwin, New York.

MATISSE: Mlle. Yvonne Landsberg, 1914. Oil, 57¼ x 42". Collection Mr. and Mrs. Walter C. Arensberg, Hollywood.

MATISSE: Lorette, 1916. Oil on wood, 21 x 18". The Lewisohn Collection, New York.

ROUSSEAU: Joseph Brummer, 1909. Oil, 45¾ x 35″. Collection Dr. Franz Meyer, Zürich. On extended loan to the Museum of Modern Art, New York.

above: de CHIRICO: Self Portrait, 1908. Oil, 28¼ x 21⅝". Collection Miss Ann Resor, Greenwich, Connecticut.

below: HODLER: James Vibert, Sculptor, 1907. Oil, 25 x 25". The Art Institute of Chicago, Helen Birch Bartlett Memorial Collection.

de CHIRICO: The Child's Brain, 1914. Oil, 32 x 25½". Collection André Breton, Paris. Not in the exhibition.

DUCHAMP: The Artist's Father, 1910. Oil, 36½ x 29". Collection Mr. and Mrs. Walter C. Arensberg, Hollywood.

DUCHAMP: The Sonata (the artist's mother and three sisters), 1911. Oil, 56½ x 44¼". Collection Mr. and Mrs. Walter C. Arensberg, Hollywood.

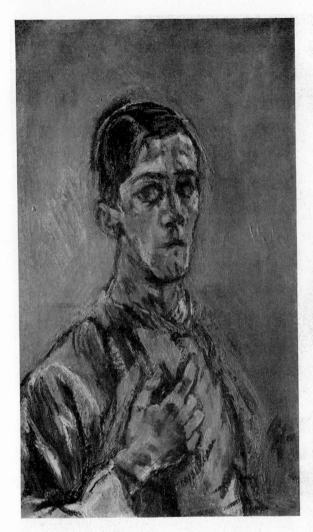

above: KOKOSCHKA: Self Portrait, 1913. Oil, 32¼ x 19¾". The Museum of Modern Art, New York. Purchase Fund.

below: HARKAVY: Oskar Kokoschka, 1932. Plaster, 12½" high. Lent by the artist.

KOKOSCHKA: Egon Wellesz, 1911. Oil, 29¼ x 27". Buchholz Gallery, New York.   **63**

CHAGALL: The Rabbi of Vitebsk, 1914. Oil, 46 x 35". The Art Institute of Chicago, Joseph Winterbotham Collection.

CHAGALL: Double Portrait (the artist and his wife), 1917. Oil, 95 x 55". Pierre Matisse Gallery, New York.

MODIGLIANI: Double Portrait (M. and Mme. Jacques Lipchitz), 1916–1917. Oil, 31⅞ x 21¼". The
Art Institute of Chicago, Helen Birch Bartlett Memorial Collection.

above: LIPCHITZ: Mme. Lipchitz, 1922. Bronze. Collection the artist. Not in the exhibition.
below: Snapshot of Jacques Lipchitz, Maria Gutierrez Blanchard and Mme. Lipchitz, c. 1917.

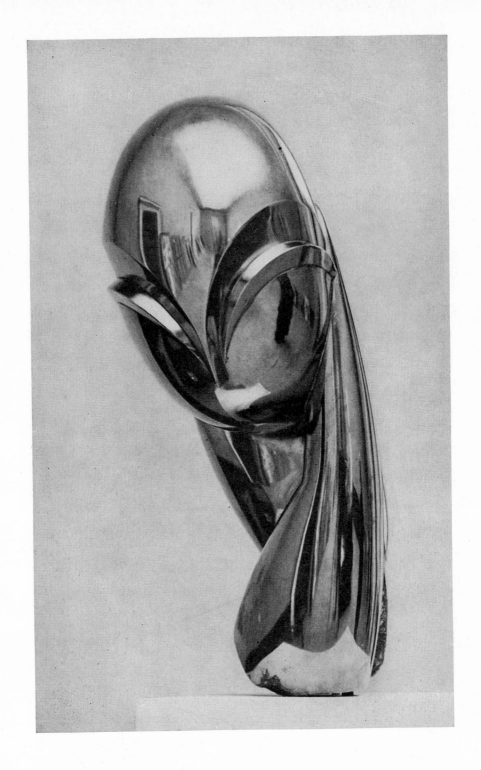

above: BRANCUSI: Mlle. Pogany, 1920. Polished bronze, 17½″ high. Albright Art Gallery, Buffalo.

color plate: MODIGLIANI: Woman with a Necklace (Lolotte), 1917. Oil, 36⅜ x 24¾″. Collection Charles H. Worcester, Chicago.

ROUAULT: Henri Lebasque, 1917. Oil, 36¼ x 29⅞″. The Museum of Modern Art, New York. Purchase Fund.

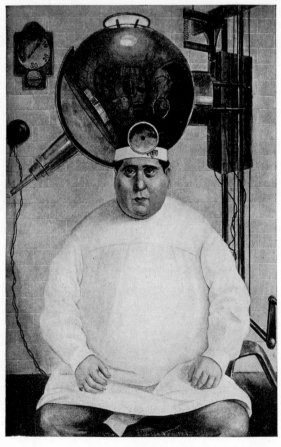

above: DIX: Self Portrait, 1912. Oil on wood, 28¾ x 19¾". Private collection.
below: DIX: Dr. Meyer-Hermann, 1926. Oil on wood, 58¾ x 39". The Museum of Modern Art, New York. Gift of Philip Johnson.

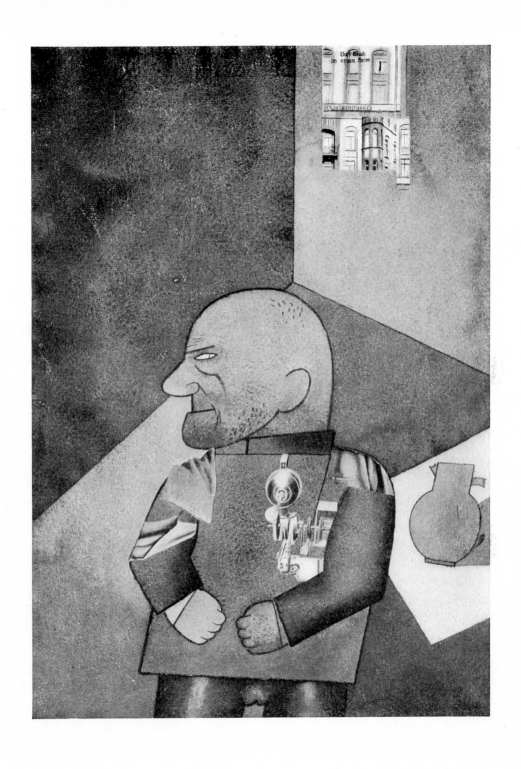

GROSZ: The Engineer Heartfield, 1920. Watercolor and collage, 16 x 11½". Collection A. Conger Goodyear, New York.

above: BECKMANN: Self Portrait as a Sailor, 1926. Oil, 39 x 27". J. B. Neumann, New York.

below: BECKMANN: Self Portrait, 1932. Woodcut, 8¾ x 6⅛". The Museum of Modern Art, New York.
Anonymous gift.

above: KOLLWITZ: Self Portrait, 1930. Drawing, 14¼ x 13¼". Collection Erich Cohn, New York.
below left: KOLLWITZ: Self Portrait, 1934. Lithograph, 11½ x 8½". Buchholz Gallery, New York.
below right: KOLLWITZ: Self Portrait, 1936. Bronze, 14½" high. Collection Erich Cohn, New York.

above: JOHN: Col. T. E. Lawrence, D. S. O., c. 1919. Oil, 18 x 15". Collection William P. Clyde, Jr.,
courtesy of the Yale University Art Gallery, New Haven, Connecticut.
below: KENNINGTON: Col. T. E. Lawrence (Aircraftsman Shaw, R. A. F.), 1927. Bronze, 19" high. Lent
by the artist. On extended loan to The Museum of Modern Art, New York.

JOHN: Marchesa Casati, 1918–1919. Oil, 38 x 27". The Art Gallery of Toronto, Toronto, Ontario.

above right: CANADÉ: Self Portrait with Fedora Hat, 1922.

Oil, 8 x 6". Albright Art Gallery, Buffalo.

above left: CANADÉ: Double Self Portrait,
1923.

Oil on wood, 9½ x 7¼". E. Weyhe,
New York.

below: SCARAVAGLIONE, Vincent
Canadé, 1927.

Bronze, 11½" high. Lent by the artist.

left: MAHONRI YOUNG: Alfy (Alfred H. Maurer), 1904. Patined plaster, 14″ high. Lent by the artist.
right: MAURER: Self Portrait, c. 1926. Oil on composition board, 39 x 24″. Buchholz Gallery, New
    York.

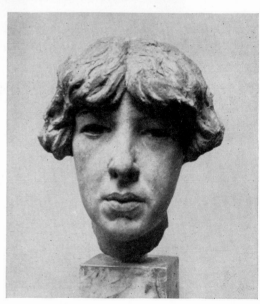

above: GUY PÈNE Du BOIS: The Opera Box (Mrs. Harry Payne Whitney), c. 1919. Oil, 20 x 25". Collection Mrs. Willard Burdette Force, New York.

below: DAVIDSON: Mask of Mrs. Harry Payne Whitney, 1910. Terra cotta, 12" high. Collection Mrs. G. McCullough Miller, Westbury, Long Island.

above left: LURÇAT: Mrs. Chester Dale, 1928. Oil, 47 x 27¾". Chester Dale Collection, New York.

above right: BELLOWS: Mrs. Chester Dale, 1919. Oil, 41¾ x 39¾". Chester Dale Collection, New York.

below: LÉGER: Mrs. Chester Dale, 1935. Oil, 41¼ x 31⅜". Chester Dale Collection, New York.

STETTHEIMER: My Sister, 1923. Oil, 40 x 26". Lent by the artist.

above left: ROUAULT: M. Thérèse Bonney, 1932. (Profile) Mixed medium on paper, 24¼ x 17⅛".
above right: ROUAULT: M. Thérèse Bonney, 1932. (Full face) Mixed medium on paper, 15 x 10¾".
below left: LURÇAT: M. Thérèse Bonney. Oil, 39¾ x 31¼".
below right: DUFY: M. Thérèse Bonney, 1938. Oil, 45½ x 31¼".
All collection of Miss M. Thérèse Bonney, New York.

LUKS: Sassafras (Eleanor), 1927. Oil, 30 x 25". Museum of Art, Rhode Island School of Design, Providence.

ORPEN: Roland Knoedler, 1922. Oil, 33½ x 30". Collection Mr. and Mrs. Charles R. Henschel, New York.

PICASSO: The Reply (Mme. Picasso), 1923. Oil, 41 x 32″. Paul Rosenberg and Company, New York.

above: MATISSE: Dr. Claribel Cone, 1933–34. Charcoal drawing, 23¼ x 16″. Collection Miss Etta
      Cone, Baltimore.
below: PICASSO: Dr. Claribel Cone, 1922. Pencil drawing, 25¼ x 19¼″. Collection Miss Etta Cone,
      Baltimore.

above: LACHAISE: George L. K. Morris, 1933. Marble, 32⅛″ high. Collection George L. K. Morris, New York.

below: LACHAISE: Woman Walking (Mrs. Gaston Lachaise), 1922. Bronze, 18½″ high. The Museum of Modern Art, New York. Anonymous gift.

LACHAISE: John Marin, 1927. Bronze, 11″ high. The Museum of Modern Art, New York. Gift of Mrs. John D. Rockefeller, Jr.

WEBER: Self Portrait, 1928. Oil, 17 x 15". Lent by the artist.

above: SOUTINE: Mme. Marcel Castaing, c.1928. Oil, 39⅜ x 27⅞". Collection Miss Adelaide M. de Groot. On extended loan to The Museum of Modern Art, New York.

below: Mme. Marcel Castaing. Photograph.

BELLOWS: Lady Jean (the artist's daughter), 1924. Oil, 72 x 36". Collection Stephen C. Clark, New York.

SPEICHER: Katherine Cornell as Candida, 1925–26. Oil, 84 x 44½". The Museum of Modern Art, New York. Gift of Miss Katherine Cornell.

above: LEWIS: T. S. Eliot, 1938. Oil, 30 x 20". Collection Mr. and Mrs. Stanley Rogers Resor, Columbus, Georgia.

below: KAUFFER: T. S. Eliot, 1938–1939. Photograph. Lent by the photographer.

above: EPSTEIN: John Dewey, 1927. Bronze, 21″ high. Collection Teachers College Library, Columbia
    University, New York.
below: SCHMID: John Dewey, 1931. Mosaic, 20 x 16″. J. B. Neumann, New York.

above: SHAHN: Gov. Rolph of California, 1931–1932. Gouache, 15¾ x 11¾". Lent by the artist.
below: SHAHN: Bartolomeo Vanzetti and Nicola Sacco, 1932. Gouache, 10½ x 14½". The Museum
of Modern Art, New York. Gift of Mrs. John D. Rockefeller, Jr.

KUHN: The Man From Eden (George Fitzgerald), 1930. Oil, 30 x 25". Collection Mrs. T. G. Kenefick, Buffalo.

BROOK: George Biddle Playing the Flute, 1929. Oil, 40⅜ x 30¼". The Museum of Modern Art, New York. Gift of Mrs. John D. Rockefeller, Jr.

above left: BIDDLE: Woman with a Letter (Marguerite Zorach), 1933. Oil, 32 x 26". Metropolitan
   Museum of Art, New York.

above right: William ZORACH: Mrs. William Zorach, 1924. Pink marble, 18" high. Lent by the artist.

below right: LYNES: Mr. and Mrs. William Zorach, 1934. Photograph.

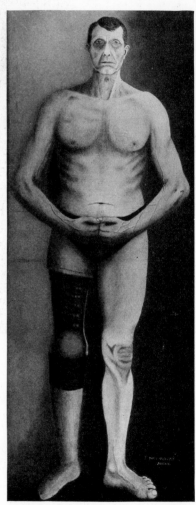

above left: KANE: Self Portrait, 1929. Oil, 36½ x 27½". The Museum of Modern Art, New York. Mrs. John D. Rockefeller, Jr. Purchase Fund.

below right: KANE: Self Portrait, before 1929. Oil, 72 x 30". This picture was later covered by another portrait, Brother Patrick in the Uniform of the Black Watch. Collection Walter P. Chrysler, Jr. Not in the exhibition.

below left: John Kane, 1929. Photograph. Courtesy of Sidney Janis, New York.

above: WOOD: American Gothic (Mrs. Nan Wood Graham, the artist's sister, and Dr. B. H. McKeeby), 1930. Oil on beaverboard, 29⅞ x 25″. The Art Institute of Chicago, Friends of American Art Collection.

below: Mrs. Nan Wood Graham and Dr. B. H. McKeeby. Photograph Wide World.

above: BALTHUS: André Derain, 1936. Oil, 44⅜ x 23⅜". Collection Mr. and Mrs. Stanley Rogers
Resor, Columbus, Georgia.

below: DERAIN: Self Portrait with a Pipe, 1913–14(?). Oil, 19 x 11½". Dikran G. Kelekian, Inc., New
York.

DERAIN: Girl with Pears (the artist's niece), 1939. Oil, 36 x 28¼". Collection Mr. and Mrs. Seymour H. Knox, Buffalo.

above: MIRO: Self Portrait, 1938. Pencil and oil on canvas, 57½ x 38¼". Collection Pierre
Matisse, New York.

color plate: BALTHUS: Joan Miro and his Daughter Dolores, 1937–38. Oil, 51¼ x 35". The Museum
of Modern Art, New York. Mrs. John D. Rockefeller, Jr. Purchase Fund.

above: TCHELITCHEW: Joella Lloyd, 1937. Gouache, 23⅜ x 19⅜". Collection Miss Agnes Rindge, Poughkeepsie, New York.

below left: DALI: Joella Lloyd, 1934. Painted plaster, 15½" high. Collection Miss Joella Lloyd, New York.

below right: CAMPIGLI: Joella Lloyd, 1931. Oil, 17½ x 14½". Collection Edgar A. Levy, New York.

BERARD: On the Beach (Double Self Portrait), 1933. Oil, 31¾ x 45½". Collection James Thrall Soby,
New York.

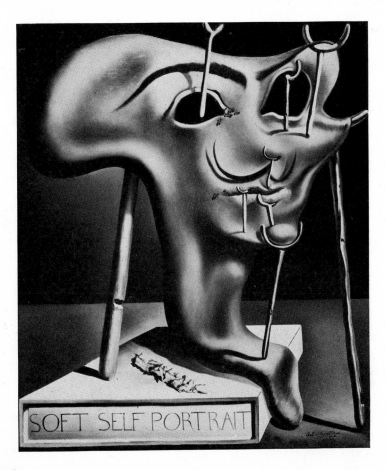

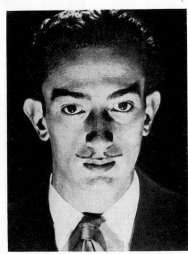

above: DALI: Soft Self Portrait, 1941. Oil, 24 x 20⅛". Lent by the artist.

below: MAN RAY: Salvador Dali, 1932. Photograph. The Museum of Modern Art, New York. Gift of
James Thrall Soby.

VAN DONGEN: E. Berry Wall, 1938. Oil, 38½ x 28½". Carnegie Institute, Pittsburgh.

POOR: The Chess Game (the artist's son Peter and daughter Anne), 1940. Oil, 36 x 30". Frank K. M. Rehn Gallery, New York.

above: DESPIAU: Antoinette Schulte, 1934. Bronze, 18¾″ high. Collection Miss Antoinette Schulte, New York.

below: NOGUCHI: George Gershwin, 1929. Bronze, 15″ high. Collection Mrs. Rose Gershwin, New York.

above: DESPIAU: Anne Morrow Lindbergh, 1939. Bronze, 15½″ high. The Museum of Modern Art, New York. Gift of Col. and Mrs. Charles A. Lindbergh.

below: BAIZERMAN: A Young Woman (Travka de Prume), 1936. Hammered copper, 14″ high. Lent by the artist.

LEVI: Margaret Boni Plays the Recorder, 1940. Oil, 21 x 15". Downtown Gallery, New York.

above: RAPHAEL SOYER: The Artist's Parents, 1932. Oil, 26 x 28″. Lent by the artist.

below left: RAPHAEL SOYER: Self Portrait in the Second Year of the War, 1941. Oil, 15 x 10″. Associated American Artists, New York.

below right: GERSHOY: Raphael Soyer, 1939. Plaster, 20⅛″ high. Lent by the artist.

LIBERTÉ: The Artist's Wife, 1942. Oil, 50 x 30". Babcock Galleries, New York.

MOMMER: The Evening Meal (the artist's family), 1941–42. Oil, 50 x 75". Lent by the artist.

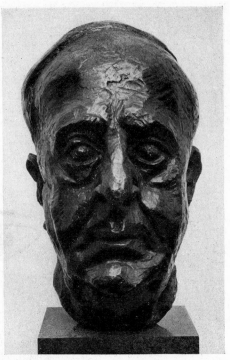

above left: LIPCHITZ: Marsden Hartley, 1942. Bronze, 22″ high (side view). Buchholz Gallery, New York.

above right: LIPCHITZ: Marsden Hartley, 1942. Bronze, 22″ high.

below: LIPCHITZ: Marsden Hartley Sleeping, 1942. Terra cotta, 14½″ high. Buchholz Gallery, New York.

HARTLEY: Adelard the Drowned, 1938–39. Oil on academy board, 28 x 22″. Collection Mr. and Mrs. Hudson D. Walker, Forest Hills, Long Island.

above: WATKINS: Thomas Raeburn White, 1940. Oil, 34½ x 45″. Collection Thomas Raeburn White, Philadelphia.

color plate: WATKINS: The Misses Maude and Maxine Meyer de Schauensee and Muffin, 1941. Oil, 50 x 40⅛″. Collection Mr. and Mrs. R. Meyer de Schauensee, Devon, Pennsylvania.

PICASSO: Dora Maar, 1937. Oil, 21⅝ x 18⅛". Bignou Gallery, New York.

TCHELITCHEW: Lincoln Kirstein, 1937. Oil, 44 x 36". Collection Lincoln Kirstein, New York.

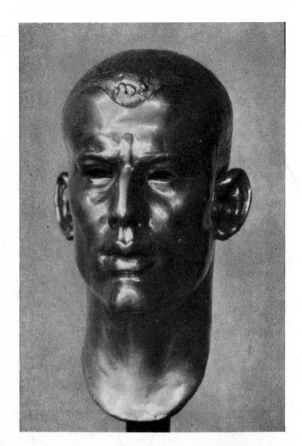

above: LACHAISE: Lincoln Kirstein, 1932. Bronze, 15½″ high. Collection Lincoln Kirstein, New York.
below: CHARLOT: Lincoln Kirstein, 1932. Oil, 19¼ x 15¼″. Collection Lincoln Kirstein, New York.

above: EPSTEIN: Albert Einstein, 1933. Bronze, 17¼″ high. Collection Hiram J. Halle, New York.
below: JACOBI: Albert Einstein, 1938. Photograph. Lent by the photographer.

120

above: ZADKINE: André Gide, 1942. Plaster, 35″ high. Lent by the artist.
below: LYNES: André Gide, 1932. Photograph. Lent by the photographer.

above: ERNST: Leonora in the Morning Light, 1940. Oil, 25½ x 31½". Collection Miss Leonora Carrington, New York.

below: CARRINGTON: Self Portrait. 1940. Oil, 25½ x 31½". Collection Max Ernst, New York.

DELVAUX: Woman before a Mirror, 1936. Oil. Collection Gordon Onslow-Ford, New York.

ALBRIGHT: "And God Created Man in His Own Image" (George Washington Stafford), 1930–31.
Oil, 48¼ x 26⅛". Lent by the artist.

124

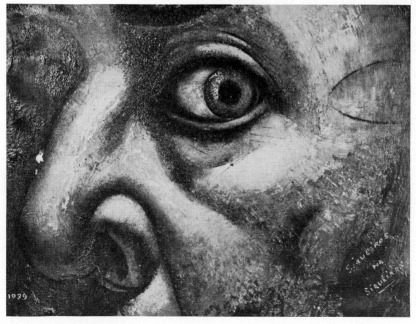

above: OROZCO: Self Portrait, 1940. Tempera on paper, 20½ x 23⅞". The Museum of Modern Art, New York.

below: SIQUEIROS: Self Portrait, 1939. Duco on board, 17 x 23⅝". Pierre Matisse Gallery, New York.

above: OROZCO: Sra. Gurza, 1942. Oil, 27⅛ x 24". Lent by the artist.

below: GALVAN: Sra. Gurza, 1942. Oil, 36 x 28". Lent by the artist.

above: RIVERA: Guadalupe Marín, 1938. Oil, 67⅛ x 47⅝″. Lent by the artist.
below: KAHLO: Self Portrait, 1941. Oil, 20 x 15⅛″. Lent by the artist.

above: PORTINARI: Rockwell Kent, 1937. Oil on canvas, 22 x 18". Collection Rockwell Kent, Ausable
    Forks, New York.

below: MEZA: Self Portrait, 1942. Oil on paper, 20½ x 17½". Lent by the artist.

above: AVERY: March Avery (the artist's daughter), 1942. Oil, 36 x 28". Valentine Gallery of Modern Art, New York.

below: HIRSHFIELD: Tailor-made Girl (the artist's daughter), 1939. Oil, 41⅛ x 25⅛". Collection Sidney Janis, New York.

CADMUS: Lloyd and Barbara Wescott with Eclipse of Morston, Mulhocaway Butterfat Favorite and Heartsease Butterfat Heather, 1942. Egg tempera on wood, 21¾ x 35". Collection Mr. and Mrs. Lloyd Bruce Wescott, Mulhocaway Farm, Clinton, New Jersey.

HIRSCH: W. Somerset Maugham, 1942. Oil, 30⅛ x 44″. Lent by the artist.

BERMAN: Night Music (imaginary portrait of Ona Munson), 1941. Oil, 52 x 39". Collection Jere Abbott, Northampton, Massachusetts.

Titles preceded by an asterisk * are reproduced in this book. In dimensions, height precedes width.

ABBOTT, Berenice. American, born 1898.

Marie Laurencin, c.1926. Photograph. Lent by the photographer.

James Joyce, 1928. Photograph. Lent by the photographer.

Reuven Rubin, 1942. Photograph. Lent by the photographer.

ALBRIGHT, Ivan LeLorraine. American, born 1897.

*"And God Created Man in His Own Image" (George Washington Stafford), 1930–31. Oil on canvas, 48¼ x 26⅛". Lent by the artist. (Plate page 124)

ANDRÉ, Albert. French, born 1869.

*Renoir in his Studio, 1916. Oil on canvas, 19¾ x 24". Durand-Ruel, New York. (Plate page 39)

ANGUIANO, Raúl. Mexican, born 1909.

María Asúnsolo, 1942. Oil on canvas, 39½ x 31½". Lent by the artist.

ANONYMOUS. American.

John Kane, 1929. Photograph. Courtesy Sidney Janis, New York.

AVERY, Milton. American, born 1893.

*March Avery (the artist's daughter), 1942. Oil on canvas, 36 x 28". Valentine Gallery of Modern Art, New York. (Plate page 129)

BAIZERMAN, Saul. American, born Russia 1889.

*A Young Woman (Travka de Prume), 1936. Hammered copper, 14" high. Lent by the artist. (Plate page 109)

BALTHUS (Balthasar Klossowsky). French, born 1910.

*André Derain, 1936. Oil on canvas, 44⅜ x 23⅜". Collection Mr. and Mrs. Stanley Rogers Resor, Columbus, Georgia. (Plate page 100)

*Joan Miro and his Daughter Dolores, 1937–38. Oil on canvas, 51¼ x 35". The Museum of Modern Art, Mrs. John D. Rockefeller, Jr., Purchase Fund. (Color plate facing page 102)

The Bernese Hat (Mme. Balthus), c.1938. Oil on canvas, 36⅛ x 28⅝". The Wadsworth Atheneum, Hartford, Connecticut.

BARTHÉ, Richmond. American, born 1901.

Edgar Kaufmann, Jr., 1939. Original plaster, 12¼" high. Lent by the artist.

BECKMANN, Max. German, born 1884. Now in Holland.

*Self-Portrait as a Sailor, 1926. Oil on canvas, 39 x 27". J. B. Neumann, New York. (Plate page 72)

*Self-Portrait, 1932. Woodcut, 8¾ x 6⅛". The Museum of Modern Art, anonymous gift. (Plate page 72)

BELLOWS, George W. American, 1882–1925.

*Mrs. Chester Dale, 1919. Oil on canvas, 42¾ x 39¾". Chester Dale Collection, New York. (Plate page 79)

133

*Lady Jean (the artist's daughter), 1924. Oil on canvas, 72 x 36". Collection Stephen C. Clark, New York. (Plate page 90)

BÉRARD, Christian. French, born 1902.

*On the Beach (double self-portrait), 1933. Oil on canvas, 31¾ x 45½". Collection James Thrall Soby, New York. (Plate page 104)

BERMAN, Eugene. American, born Russia 1899.

*Night Music (imaginary portrait of Ona Munson), 1941. Oil on canvas, 52 x 39". Collection Jere Abbott, Northampton, Massachusetts. (Plate page 132)

BERNI, Antonio. Argentine, born 1908.

Chico, 1942. Oil on canvas, 37 x 22⅝". Lent anonymously.

BIDDLE, George. American, born 1885.

*Woman with a Letter (Marguerite Zorach), 1933. Oil on canvas, 32 x 26". The Metropolitan Museum of Art, New York. (Plate page 97)

BOLDINI, Giovanni. Italian, 1845–1931.

*Miss Edith Blair, 1902. Oil on canvas, 57¾ x 36½". Collection Miss Edith Blair, Marseille, France. (Plate page 35)

BONNARD, Pierre. French, born 1867.

*The Checkered Dress (Mme. Bonnard), 1928. Oil on canvas, 30⅞ x 18⅝". Collection Laurance S. Rockefeller, New York. (Plate page 44)

BOUGHTON, Alice. American, born 1866.

Albert Pinkham Ryder, c.1903. Photograph. Lent by the photographer.

BRANCUSI, Constantin. Rumanian, born 1876. Lives in France.

*Mlle. Pogany, 1920. Polished bronze, 17½" high. Albright Art Gallery, Buffalo, New York. (Plate page 68)

BROOK, Alexander. American, born 1898.

*George Biddle Playing the Flute, 1929. Oil on canvas, 40⅜ x 30¼". The Museum of Modern Art, gift of Mrs. John D. Rockefeller, Jr. (Plate page 96)

Mrs. John Hay Whitney, 1942. Oil on canvas, 14 x 10". Collection Mr. and Mrs. John Hay Whitney, New York.

CADMUS, Paul. American, born 1906.

*Lloyd and Barbara Wescott, with Eclipse of Morston, Mulhocaway Butterfat Favorite and Heartsease Butterfat Heather, 1942. Egg tempera on panel, 21¾ x 35". Collection Mr. and Mrs. Lloyd Bruce Wescott, Clinton, New Jersey. (Plate page 130)

Donald Windham, 1941. Pencil drawing, 11 x 9". Collection Donald Windham, New York.

CAMPIGLI, Massimo. Italian, born 1895.

*Joella Lloyd, 1931. Oil on canvas, 17½ x 14½". Collection Edgar A. Levy, New York. (Plate page 103)

CANADÉ, Vincent. American, born Italy 1879.

*Self-Portrait with Fedora Hat, 1922. Oil on canvas, 8 x 6". Albright Art Gallery, Buffalo, New York. (Plate page 76)

*Double Self-Portrait, 1923. Oil on wood, 9½ x 7¼". Collection E. Weyhe, New York. (Plate page 76)

Self-Portrait, c.1926. Oil on canvas, 18⅝ x 14". The Museum of Modern Art, gift of Mrs. John D. Rockefeller, Jr.

CARRINGTON, Leonora. British, born 1917.

*Self-Portrait, 1940. Oil on canvas, 25½ x 31½". Collection Max Ernst, New York. (Plate page 122)

Max Ernst, 1940. Oil on canvas, 20 x 10". Collection Max Ernst, New York.

CARROLL, John. American, born 1892.

Brigitta Valentiner, 1942. Oil on canvas, 16 x 14". Collection Frank K. M. Rehn, New York.

CASTELLÓN, Federico. *American, born Spain 1914.*

Nocturnal Pilgrimage (triple self-portrait with imaginary figures), 1940. Oil on canvas, 24 x 36". Associated American Artists, Inc., New York.

CHAGALL, Marc. *Russian, born 1887. Now in U. S. A.*

*The Rabbi of Vitebsk, 1914. Oil on canvas, 46 x 35". The Art Institute of Chicago, Joseph Winterbotham Collection. (Plate page 64)

*Double Portrait (the artist and his wife), 1917. Oil on canvas, 92½ x 54". Pierre Matisse Gallery, New York. (Plate page 65)

Charlie Chaplin, 1929. Ink drawing, 16⅜ x 11⅛". Buchholz Gallery, New York.

CHARLOT, Jean. *American, born France 1898.*

*Lincoln Kirstein, 1932. Oil on canvas, 19¼ x 15¼". Collection Lincoln Kirstein, New York. (Plate page 119)

De CHIRICO, Giorgio. *Italian, born Greece 1888.*

*Self-Portrait, 1908. Oil on canvas, 28¼ x 21⅝". Collection Miss Ann Resor, Greenwich, Connecticut. (Plate page 58)

CORDES, Paul. *American, born Germany 1893.*

Anne Morrow Lindbergh. Photograph. Lent by the photographer.

CORNELL, Joseph. *American, born 1904.*

Greta Garbo in "The Crystal Mask," 1940–42. Photomontage, 14¼ x 9¾". Lent by the artist.

CUSHING, Lily. *American, born 1909.*

Paula Laurence, 1942. Oil on canvas, 22 x 17". Lent by the artist.

DALI, Salvador. *Spanish, born 1904.*

*Joella Lloyd, 1934. Painted plaster, 15½" high. Collection Miss Joella Lloyd, New York. (Plate page 103)

Portrait of Gala (Mme. Dali), 1935. Oil on wood. 12¾ x 10½". The Museum of Modern Art, anonymous gift.

Dr. Sigmund Freud, 1938. Ink, 12 x 10½". Collection Edward James, South Laguna, California.

Harpo Marx, 1939. Pencil, 16¼ x 12¾". Collection Lieut. Henry P. McIlhenny, U.S.N.R., Philadelphia, Pennsylvania.

*Soft Self-Portrait, 1941. Oil on canvas, 24 x 20⅛". Lent by the artist. (Plate page 105)

DAVIDSON, Jo. *American, born 1883.*

*Mask of Mrs. Harry Payne Whitney, 1910. Terra cotta, 8¾" high. Collection Mrs. G. McCullough Miller, Westbury, Long Island, New York. (Plate page 78)

La Pasionaria (Dolores Ibarruri), 1938. Bronze, 20½" high. The Museum of Modern Art.

DELVAUX, Paul. *Belgian, born 1897.*

*Woman before a Mirror, 1936. Oil on canvas, 43¼ x 53⅛". Collection Gordon Onslow-Ford, courtesy of André Breton, New York. (Plate page 123)

DE MARTINI, Joseph. *American, born 1896.*

Self-Portrait, 1940. Oil on canvas, 37 x 26". The Macbeth Gallery, New York.

DERAIN, André. *French, born 1880.*

*Self-Portrait with a Pipe, 1913–14(?). Oil on canvas, 19 x 11½". Dikran G. Kelekian, Inc., New York. (Plate page 100)

*Girl with Pears (the artist's niece), 1939. Oil on canvas, 36 x 28¼". Collection Mr. and Mrs. Seymour H. Knox, Buffalo, New York. (Plate page 101)

DESPIAU, Charles. *French, born 1880.*

Mme. Othon Friesz, 1924. Original plaster, 20⅞" high. The Museum of Modern Art, gift of Mrs. John D. Rockefeller, Jr.

*Antoinette Schulte, 1934. Bronze, 20" high. Collection Miss Antoinette Schulte, New York. (Plate page 108)

135

*Anne Morrow Lindbergh, 1939. Bronze, 15½"
high. The Museum of Modern Art, gift of Col.
and Mrs. Charles A. Lindbergh. (Plate page
109)

DIX, Otto. German, born 1891.

*Self-Portrait, 1912. Oil on wood, 28¾ x 19¾".
Lent anonymously. (Plate page 70)

*Dr. Meyer-Hermann, 1926. Oil on wood, 58¾
x 39". The Museum of Modern Art, gift of
Philip Johnson. (Plate page 70)

DLUGOSZ, Louis. American, born 1916.

Henry Dlugosz (the artist's brother), 1938.
Terra cotta, 12½" high. The Museum of Modern Art, Purchase Fund.

Du BOIS, Guy Pène. American, born 1884.

*The Opera Box (Mrs. Harry Payne Whitney),
c.1919. Oil on canvas, 20 x 25". Collection
Mrs. Willard Burdette Force, New York. (Plate
page 78)

DUCHAMP, Marcel. French, born 1887. Now in
U. S. A.

*The Artist's Father, 1910. Oil on canvas, 36½
x 29". Collection Mr. and Mrs. Walter C.
Arensberg, Hollywood, California. (Plate page
60)

*The Sonata (the artist's mother and three
sisters), 1911. Oil on canvas, 57 x 44¼".
Collection Mr. and Mrs. Walter C. Arensberg,
Hollywood, California. (Plate page 61)

DUFY, Raoul. French, born 1879.

*Miss M. Thérèse Bonney, 1938. Oil on canvas,
45¾ x 32". Collection Miss M. Thérèse
Bonney, New York. (Plate page 81)

EAKINS, Thomas. American, 1844-1916.

Self-Portrait, c.1902. Oil on canvas, 30 x 25".
National Academy of Design, New York.

*Miss Elizabeth L. Burton, 1906. Oil on canvas,
30 x 25". The Minneapolis Institute of Arts,
Minneapolis, Minnesota. (Plate page 33)

ELISOFON, Eliot. American, born 1911.

José Clemente Orozco, 1940. Photograph. The
Museum of Modern Art, gift of the photographer.

ENSOR, Baron James. Belgian, born 1860.

Self-Portrait, 1915. Pastel, 9½ x 7". Nierendorf
Gallery, New York.

Self-Portrait, 1937. Oil on wood, 12½ x 9½".
Collection Sam Salz, New York.

EPSTEIN, Jacob. American, born 1880. Lives in
London.

Oriol Ross, 1932. Bronze, 25" high. The Museum of Modern Art, gift of Edward M. M.
Warburg.

*John Dewey, 1927. Bronze, 21" high. Collection
Teachers College Library, Columbia University,
New York. (Plate page 93)

*Albert Einstein, 1933. Bronze, 17¼" high. Col-
lection Hiram J. Halle, New York. (Plate page
120)

ERNST, Max. German, born 1891. Now in U. S. A.

*Leonora in the Morning Light, 1940. Oil on
canvas, 25½ x 31½". Collection Miss Leonora
Carrington, New York. (Plate page 122)

EVANS, Walker. American, born 1903.

Lincoln Kirstein, 1932. Photograph. Collection
Lincoln Kirstein, New York.

FAGGI, Alfeo. American, born 1885.

Yone Noguchi, 1919. Bronze, 18½" high.
Addison Gallery of American Art, Phillips
Academy, Andover, Massachusetts.

FORBES, Donald. American, born 1906.

José (José Limon), 1940. Oil on canvas, 19 x 15".
The Museum of Modern Art, Mrs. Simon Gug-
genheim Fund.

FRENCH, Jared. American, born 1905.

Margaret French, 1942. Egg yolk on linen-
covered composition board, 4⅝ x 5¾". Lent
by the artist.

GALVAN, Jesús Guerrero. Mexican, born 1910.

    *Sra. Gurza, 1942. Oil on canvas, 36 x 28". Lent by the artist. (Plate page 126)

GERSHOY, Eugenie. American, born Russia 1903.

    *Raphael Soyer, 1939. Original plaster, 20⅛" high. Lent by the artist. (Plate page 111)

    Carl Walters. Original plaster, 17½" high. Lent by the artist.

GLACKENS, William J. American, 1870–1938.

    *Family Group (Irene Dimock, Mrs. William J. Glackens, Ira Glackens, Mrs. D. H. Morgan), 1910. Oil on canvas, 72 x 84". Collection Mrs. William J. Glackens, New York. (Plate page 47)

GORKY, Arshile. American, born Russia 1904.

    My Sister, Ahko, 1917. Oil on canvas, 19 x 15". Lent by the artist.

GROPPER, William. American, born 1897.

    The Cigar Maker (Fernando). Oil on canvas, 16 x 24". Fogg Museum of Art, Cambridge, Massachusetts. Paul J. Sachs Collection.

GROSZ, George. American, born Germany 1893.

    *The Engineer Heartfield, 1920. Watercolor and collage, 16 x 11½". Collection A. Conger Goodyear, New York. (Plate page 71)

    My Friend E. C. (Erich Cohn), 1934. Oil on canvas, 36½ x 29". Collection Erich Cohn, New York.

HALLER, Hermann. Swiss, born 1880.

    Marie Laurencin. Terra cotta, 10" high. Collection A. Conger Goodyear, New York.

HARKAVY, Minna. American, born Esthonia 1895.

    *Oskar Kokoschka, 1932. Original plaster, 12½" high. Lent by the artist. (Plate page 62)

HARTLEY, Marsden. American, born 1877.

    Albert Pinkham Ryder, c.1938-39. Oil on academy board, 28 x 22". The Macbeth Gallery, New York.

    *Adelard the Drowned, 1938–39. Oil on academy board, 28 x 22". Collection Mr. and Mrs. Hudson D. Walker, Forest Hills, New York. (Plate page 115)

HASELTINE, Herbert. American, born Italy 1877.

    International Polo Team, 1909 (Monte Waterbury, Harry Payne Whitney, Devereux Milburn, Larry Waterbury), 1911. Bronze, 35" high. Whitney Museum of American Art, New York.

HENRI, Robert. American, 1865–1929.

    *The Masquerade Dress (Mrs. Robert Henri), 1911. Oil on canvas, 77 x 37". Collection Miss Violet Organ, New York. (Plate page 45)

HERRERA GUEVARA, Luís. Chilean, born 1891.

    Self-Portrait, 1933. Oil on cardboard, 16⅝ x 13". Lent anonymously.

HIRSCH, Joseph. American, born 1910.

    *W. Somerset Maugham, 1942. Oil on canvas, 30⅛ x 44". Lent by the artist. (Plate page 131)

HIRSHFIELD, Morris. American, born Russian Poland 1872.

    *Tailor-made Girl (the artist's daughter), 1939. Oil on canvas, 41⅛ x 25⅛". Collection Sidney Janis, New York. (Plate page 129)

HODLER, Ferdinand. Swiss, 1853–1918.

    *James Vibert, Sculptor, 1907. Oil on canvas, 25¾ x 26⅛". The Art Institute of Chicago, Helen Birch Bartlett Memorial Collection. (Plate page 58)

HOPKINSON, Charles. American, born 1869.

    John Masefield, 1919. Oil on canvasboard, 36 x 30". Collection Mr. and Mrs. Thomas W. Lamont, New York.

JACOBI, Lotte. German, born 1896.

    *Albert Einstein, 1938. Photograph. Lent by the photographer. (Plate page 120)

JOHN, Augustus. British, born 1879.

*Marchesa Casati, 1918-1919. Oil on canvas, 38 x 27″. The Art Gallery of Toronto, Toronto, Ontario. (Plate page 75)

Col. T. E. Lawrence, D.S.O., 1919. Pencil, 12 x 9″. Collection William P. Clyde, Jr., New York, courtesy of the Yale University Art Gallery, New Haven, Connecticut.

*Col. T. E. Lawrence, D.S.O., c.1919. Oil on canvas, 18 x 15″. Collection William P. Clyde, Jr., New York, courtesy of the Yale University Art Gallery, New Haven, Connecticut. (Plate page 74)

James Joyce. 1930. Pencil drawing, 17 x 12″. American-British Art Center, New York.

KAHLO, Frida. Mexican, born 1910.

*Self-Portrait. 1941. Oil on canvas, 20 x 15⅛″. Lent by the artist. (Plate page 127)

KANE, John. American, 1860–1934.

*Self-Portrait. 1929. Oil on canvas over composition board, 36½ x 27½″. The Museum of Modern Art, Mrs. John D. Rockefeller, Jr. Purchase Fund. (Plate page 98)

KAUFFER, E. McKnight. American, born 1890.

*T. S. Eliot, 1938–1939. Photograph. Lent by the photographer. (Plate page 92)

KENNINGTON, Eric. British, born 1888.

Col. T. E. Lawrence (Aircraftsman Shaw, R.A.F.), 1927. Bronze, 19″ high. Lent by the artist. On extended loan to The Museum of Modern Art, New York. (Plate page 74)

KIRCHNER, Ernst Ludwig. German, 1880–1938.

Self-Portrait, c.1908. Oil on canvas, 20 x 16½″. Collection Curt Valentin, New York.

KNOOP, Guitou.

Katharine Cornell, 1937. Bronze, 12½″ high. Lent by the artist.

KOKOSCHKA, Oskar. Austrian-Czech, born 1886. Now in England.

Dr. Tietze and his Wife, 1909. Oil on canvas, 30⅛ x 53⅝″. The Museum of Modern Art, Mrs. John D. Rockefeller, Jr. Purchase Fund.

*Egon Wellesz, 1911. Oil on canvas, 29¼ x 27″. Buchholz Gallery, New York. (Plate page 63)

*Self-Portrait, 1913. Oil on canvas, 32⅛ x19½″. The Museum of Modern Art, Purchase Fund. (Plate page 62)

KOLLWITZ, Kaethe. German, born 1867.

*Self-Portrait, c.1930. Chalk drawing, 14¼ x 13¼″. Collection Erich Cohn, New York. (Plate page 73)

*Self-Portrait, 1934. Lithograph, 8 x 7¼″. Buchholz Gallery, New York. (Plate page 73)

*Self-Portrait, 1936. Bronze, 14½″ high. Collection Erich Cohn, New York. (Plate page 73)

KUHN, Walt. American, born 1880.

*The Man from Eden (George Fitzgerald), 1930. Oil on canvas, 30 x 25″. Collection Mrs. Theodore G. Kenefick, Buffalo, New York. (Plate page 95)

Mrs. Alfred M. Frankfurter, 1938. Oil on canvas, 10⅞ x 9″. Collection Dr. and Mrs. Alfred M. Frankfurter, New York.

KUNIYOSHI, Yasuo. American, born Japan 1893.

Spanish Soprano (Paula Laurence), 1942. Oil on canvas, 42 x 32″. The Downtown Gallery, New York.

LACHAISE, Gaston. American, born France. 1882–1935.

*Woman Walking (Mrs. Gaston Lachaise), 1922. Bronze, 18½″ high. The Museum of Modern Art, anonymous gift. (Plate page 86)

*John Marin, 1928. Bronze, 11″ high. The Museum of Modern Art, gift of Mrs. John D. Rockefeller, Jr. (Plate page 87)

Woman Standing,1932. Original plaster, 22½″ high. The Museum of Modern Art, gift of Mrs. John D. Rockefeller, Jr.

*Lincoln Kirstein, 1932. Bronze, 15½" high. Collection Lincoln Kirstein, New York. (Plate page 119)

*George L. K. Morris, 1933. Marble, 32⅛" high. Collection George L. K. Morris, New York. (Plate page 86)

LANDSHOFF, *Hermann. German, born 1905. Now in U. S. A.*

Max Ernst, 1942. Photograph. Lent by the photographer.

Leonora Carrington, 1942. Photograph. Lent by the photographer.

LAURENCIN, *Marie. French, born 1885.*

*Group of Artists (Pablo Picasso, Fernande Olivier, Guillaume Apollinaire and Marie Laurencin), 1908. Oil on canvas, 24¾ x 31⅛". Collection Miss Etta Cone, Baltimore, Maryland. (Plate page 48)

The Artist at her Easel, 1930. Oil on canvas, 29 x 22". Paul Rosenberg and Company, New York.

LÉGER, *Fernand. French, born 1881.*

*Mrs. Chester Dale, 1935. Oil on canvas, 41¼ x 31⅜". Chester Dale Collection, New York. (Plate page 79)

LÉONID (*Léonid Berman*). *French, born Russia 1896.*

Self-Portrait, 1929 (?). Oil on canvas, 24 x 15". Collection James Thrall Soby, New York.

LEVI, *Julian. American, born 1900.*

The Chef (self-portrait). Oil on canvas, 25½ x 18½". Collection Mrs. Julian Levi, New York.

*Margaret Boni Plays the Recorder, 1940. Oil on canvas, 21 x 15". The Downtown Gallery, New York. (Plate page 110)

LEWIS, *Wyndham. English, born U. S. A. 1884. Now in Canada.*

*T. S. Eliot, 1938. Oil on canvas, 30 x 20". Collection Mr. and Mrs. Stanley Rogers Resor, Columbus, Georgia. (Plate page 92)

LIBERTÉ, *L. Jean. American, born 1895.*

*The Artist's Wife, 1942. Oil on canvas, 50 x 30". Babcock Galleries, New York. (Plate page 112)

LIPCHITZ, *Jacques. French, born Lithuania 1891. Now in U. S. A.*

Sketch for portrait of Barbara Reis, 1941. Terra cotta, 16" high. Buchholz Gallery, New York.

Sketch for portrait of Marsden Hartley, 1942. Terra cotta, 19¾" high. The Metropolitan Museum of Art, New York.

*Marsden Hartley, 1942. Bronze, 22" high. Buchholz Gallery, New York (Plate page 114)

*Marsden Hartley Sleeping, 1942. Terra cotta, 14½" high. Buchholz Gallery, New York. (Plate page 114)

LUKS, *George. American, 1867–1933.*

Johann Most, the Anarchist, 1910. Gouache, 17 x 11¾". Collection Mr. and Mrs. William F. Laporte, Passaic, New Jersey.

*Sassafras (Eleanor), 1927. Oil on canvas, 29¼ x 24⅜". Museum of Art, Rhode Island School of Design, Providence, Rhode Island. (Plate page 82)

LURÇAT, *Jean. French, born 1892.*

*Mrs. Chester Dale, 1928. Oil on canvas, 47 x 27¾". Chester Dale Collection, New York. (Plate page 79)

*M. Thérèse Bonney. Oil on composition board, 41⅜ x 31¼". Collection Miss M. Thérèse Bonney, New York. (Plate page 81)

LYNES, *George Platt. American, born 1907.*

*André Gide, 1932. Photograph. Lent by the photographer. (Plate page 121)

Marc Chagall, 1941. Photograph. Lent by the photographer.

MacIVER, *Loren. American, born 1909.*

Douglas Roach, 1933. Oil on wood, 17½ x 11½". Lent by the artist.

MAILLOL, Aristide. French, born 1861.

*Auguste Renoir, 1907. Bronze, 15" high. The Museum of Modern Art, gift of Mrs. Cornelius J. Sullivan, in memory of Cornelius J. Sullivan. (Plate page 39)

Mlle. Renée Rivière, 1907. Pewter, cast II, 7½" high. Weyhe Gallery, New York.

MASSON, André. French, born 1896. Now in U.S.A.

Self-Portrait, June 1940. Watercolor, 9¾ x 9¼". Buchholz Gallery, New York.

André Breton, 1941. Ink, 18¾ x 24¾". Buchholz Gallery, New York.

MATISSE, Henri. French, born 1869.

Pierre Matisse, 1905. Bronze, 6⅛" high. Collection Pierre Matisse, New York.

The Artist's Son (Pierre Matisse), 1906. Oil on canvas, 16¼ x 13". Collection Pierre Matisse, New York.

*Woman's Head (Jane Vaderin), c.1908. Bronze, 12" high. Collection Dr. and Mrs. Harry Bakwin, New York. (Plate page 54)

*Mlle. Yvonne Landsberg, 1914. Oil on canvas, 57⅞ x 38⅜". Collection Mr. and Mrs. Walter C. Arensberg, Hollywood, California. (Plate page 55)

*Lorette, 1916. Oil on wood, 21 x 18". The Lewisohn Collection, New York. (Plate page 56)

*Dr. Claribel Cone, 1933–34. Charcoal drawing, 23¼ x 16". Collection Miss Etta Cone, Baltimore, Maryland. (Plate page 85)

Miss Etta Cone, 1933–34. Charcoal drawing, 28 x 16". Collection Miss Etta Cone, Baltimore, Maryland.

Self-Portrait, 1937. Charcoal drawing, 18½ x 15¼". Collection Miss Etta Cone, Baltimore, Maryland.

MAURER, Alfred H. American, 1868–1932.

*The Black Parasol (Miss Gabrielle), c.1901–03. Oil on canvas, 36 x 29". Buchholz Gallery, New York. (Plate page 34)

*Self-Portrait, c.1926. Oil on composition board, 39 x 24". Buchholz Gallery, New York. (Plate page 77)

MERRILD, Knud. American, born Denmark 1894.

D. H. Lawrence. Gesso-wax, 10½ x 8½". Collection Mr. and Mrs. Walter C. Arensberg, Hollywood, California.

MEZA, Guillermo. Mexican, born 1917.

The Artist's Father. Oil on composition board, 17⅞ x 15". Lent anonymously.

*Self-Portrait, 1942. Oil on paper, 20½ x 17½". Lent by the artist. (Plate page 128)

MILLER, Kenneth Hayes. American, born 1876.

Albert Pinkham Ryder, 1913. Oil on canvas, 24 x 20". Phillips Memorial Gallery, Washington, D. C.

MIRO, Joan. Spanish, born 1893.

*Self-Portrait, 1938. Pencil and oil on canvas, 57½ x 38¼". Collection Pierre Matisse, New York. (Plate page 102)

MODIGLIANI, Amedeo. Italian, 1884–1920.

*Double Portrait (M. and Mme. Jacques Lipchitz), 1916–17. Oil on canvas, 31⅞ x 21¼". The Art Institute of Chicago, Helen Birch Bartlett Memorial Collection. (Plate page 66)

The Painter Hubert, 1917. Oil on canvas, 39⅜ x 25⅝". Bignou Gallery, New York.

*Woman with a Necklace (Lolotte), 1917. Oil on canvas, 36⅜ x 23¾". Collection Charles H. Worcester, Chicago, Illinois. (Color plate facing page 68)

MOMMER, Paul. American, born Luxembourg 1899.

*The Evening Meal (the artist's family), 1941–42. Oil on canvas, 50 x 75". Lent by the artist. (Plate page 113)

MONTENEGRO, Roberto. Mexican, born 1885.

George Hoyningen-Huene, 1941. Oil on canvas, 27⅜ x 23½". Lent by the artist.

NICOLAS, Joep. Dutch, born 1897. Now in U.S.A.

D. H. Lawrence, 1930. Oil on canvas, 28½ x 23". Lent by the artist.

NOGUCHI, Isamu. American, born 1904.

*George Gershwin, 1929. Bronze, 15" high. Mrs. Rose Gershwin, New York. (Plate page 108)

A. Conger Goodyear, 1933. Terra cotta, 12" high. Collection A. Conger Goodyear, New York.

Mrs. William A. M. Burden, Jr., 1940. Stone, 30" high. Collection Mr. and Mrs. William A. M. Burden, Jr., Washington, D. C.

O'GORMAN, Juán. Mexican, born 1905.

Dorothy Elliott Ward, 1942. Oil on masonite, 24 x 18⅞". Collection Miss Ines Amor, Mexico, D. F.

ORLOFF, Chana. French, born Russia 1888.

Reuven Rubin, 1925. Bronze, 25¼" high. The Brooklyn Museum.

OROZCO, José Clemente. Mexican, born 1883.

Julia Peterkin, 1930. Oil on canvas, 21 x 15". J. B. Neumann, New York.

*Self-Portrait, 1940. Tempera on paper, 20½ x 23⅞". The Museum of Modern Art. (Plate page 125)

*Sra. Gurza, 1942. Oil on canvas, 27⅛ x 24". Lent by the artist. (Plate page 126)

ORPEN, Sir William. British, born Ireland. 1878–1931.

*Roland F. Knoedler, 1922. Oil on canvas, 36½ x 30½". Collection Mr. and Mrs. Charles R. Henschel, New York. (Plate page 83)

PASCIN, Jules. American, born Bulgaria. 1885–1930.

Hermine David. Oil on canvas, 32 x 23½". Passedoit Gallery, New York.

Hermine David. Oil on canvas, 20¼ x 15⅛". Collection A. Conger Goodyear, New York.

George Biddle and Jane Belo. Lithographic crayon drawing, 21⅛ x 19¼". The Museum of Modern Art, anonymous gift.

PICASSO, Pablo. Spanish, born 1881.

Mme. Soler. Barcelona, 1903. Oil on canvas, 40 x 28". J. K. Thannhauser, New York.

*Fernande Olivier, 1905. Bronze, 14" high. Buchholz Gallery, New York. (Plate page 48)

*Fernande, 1908. Oil on canvas, 24¼ x 16¾". Bignou Gallery, New York. (Plate page 49)

*Woman's Head, 1909 (?). Bronze, 16¼" high. The Museum of Modern Art, Mrs. John D. Rockefeller, Jr., Purchase Fund. (Plate page 48)

Georges Braque, 1909. Oil on canvas, 24¼ x 19¾". Collection Frank Crowninshield, New York.

Henry Kahnweiler, 1910. Oil on canvas, 39½ x 28⅝". Collection Mrs. Charles B. Goodspeed, Chicago.

*Dr. Claribel Cone, 1922. Pencil, 25¼ x 19¼". Collection Miss Etta Cone, Baltimore, Maryland. (Plate page 85)

*The Reply (Mme. Picasso), 1923. Oil on canvas, 40 x 32¼". Paul Rosenberg and Company, New York. (Plate page 84)

*Dora Maar, 1937. Oil on canvas, 21⅝ x 18⅛". Bignou Gallery, New York. (Plate page 117)

POOR, Henry Varnum. American, born 1888.

*The Chess Game (the artist's son Peter and daughter Anne), 1940. Oil on canvas, 36 x 30". Frank K. M. Rehn Gallery, New York. (Plate page 107)

PORTINARI, Cándido. Brazilian, born 1903.

*Rockwell Kent, 1937. Oil on canvas, 22 x 18". Collection Rockwell Kent, Ausable Forks, New York. (Plate page 128)

RAY, Man. American, born 1890.

*Salvador Dali, 1932. Photograph. The Museum of Modern Art, gift of James Thrall Soby. (Plate page 105)

André Derain, 1932. Photograph. The Museum of Modern Art, gift of James Thrall Soby.

REDON, Odilon. French, 1840–1916.

*Dream Shadows. Pastel, 19½ x 25". The Lewisohn Collection, New York. (Plate page 41)

RENOIR, Pierre Auguste. French, 1841–1919.

*Coco (the artist's youngest son, Claude), 1905. Bronze, 10¾" high. Collection Miss Mabel Choate, New York. (Plate page 38)

*Claude Renoir Painting, 1906. Oil on canvas, 21¼ x 17½". Collection Mr. and Mrs. Josiah Titzell, Georgetown, Connecticut. (Plate page 38)

*Mother and Child (Frau Thurneyssen and her daughter), 1910. Oil on canvas, 39⅜ x 31½". Albright Art Gallery, Buffalo, New York. (Plate page 42)

Young Shepherd Resting (Frau Thurneyssen's son), 1911. Oil on canvas, 28¾ x 36⅝", Durand-Ruel, New York.

*Mme. Tilla Durieux, 1914. Oil on canvas, 36½ x 29". Collection Stephen C. Clark, New York. (Color frontispiece)

RIVERA, Diego. Mexican, born 1886.

Young Man in a Grey Sweater (Jacques Lipchitz), 1914. Oil on canvas, 25⅝ x 21⅝". The Museum of Modern Art, gift of T. Catesby Jones.

Self-Portrait, 1918. Pencil drawing, 13¼ x 9". Collection Carl Zigrosser, Philadelphia, Pennsylvania.

*Guadalupe Marín, 1938. Oil on canvas, 67⅛ x 47⅝". Lent by the artist. (Plate page 127)

RODIN, Auguste. French, 1840–1917.

*Mme. X (Comtesse Mathieu de Noailles), c.1907. White marble, 19½" high. The Metropolitan Museum of Art, New York. Gift of Thomas Fortune Ryan. (Plate page 37)

*Thomas Fortune Ryan, c.1910–11. Bronze, 23" high. The Metropolitan Museum of Art, New York. Gift of the sculptor. (Plate page 37)

ROTHENSTEIN, William. British, 1859–1924.

André Gide, 1918. Sanguine and white on paper, 11 x 7⅞". Collection William N. Eisendrath, Jr., Glencoe, Illinois.

ROUAULT, Georges. French, born 1871.

*Henri Lebasque, 1917. Oil on canvas, 36¼ x 28⅞". The Museum of Modern Art, Purchase Fund. (Plate page 69)

André Suarès, c.1908. Watercolor, 12¼ x 7¾". The Weyhe Gallery, New York.

*M. Thérèse Bonney, 1932. (Full face.) Mixed medium on canvas covered board, 15 x 10¾". Collection Miss M. Thérèse Bonney, New York. (Plate page 81)

*M. Thérèse Bonney, 1932. (Left profile.) Mixed medium on paper, 24¾ x 17⅝". (Right profile on reverse of paper.) Collection Miss M. Thérèse Bonney, New York. (Plate page 81)

ROUSSEAU, Henri. French, 1844–1910.

*Joseph Brummer, 1909. Oil, 45¾ x 35". Collection Dr. F. Meyer, Zürich, Switzerland, on extended loan to The Museum of Modern Art. (Plate page 57)

RUBIN, Reuven. Palestinian, born Rumania 1893. Now in U. S. A.

Self-Portrait, 1936–1939. Oil on canvas, 46 x 35⅜". Lent by the artist.

SARGENT, John Singer. American, 1856–1925.

*Mrs. Fiske Warren and her Daughter, 1903. Oil on canvas, 60 x 40½". Collection Mrs. Warren Lothrop, Cambridge, Massachusetts. (Plate page 36)

William Butler Yeats, 1908. Charcoal drawing, 24 x 17⅞". Collection Stephen C. Clark, New York.

Charles Deering in Florida, 1917. Oil on canvas, 28¼ x 22¼". Collection Mr. and Mrs. Chauncey McCormick, Chicago.

Charles Deering. Charcoal drawing, 9½ x 6⅝". Collection Mrs. Richard E. Danielson, courtesy Museum of Fine Arts, Boston, Massachusetts.

SCARAVAGLIONE, Concetta. American, born 1900.

*Vincent Canadé, 1927 (?). Bronze, 11½" high. Lent by the artist. (Plate page 76)

SCHMID, Elsa. American, born 1897.

*John Dewey, 1931. Mosaic, 20 x 16". J. B. Neumann, New York. (Plate page 93)

SCHNAKENBURG, Henry. American, born 1892.

Gerald McCann, 1931. Oil on canvas, 36 x 24¼". Collection Mrs. Willard Burdette Force, New York.

SELIGMANN, Kurt. Swiss, born 1900. Now in U. S. A.

After-image of André Masson, 1942. Oil on glass, 15 x 11¾". Lent by the artist.

SHAHN, Ben. American, born Russia 1898.

*Governor Rolph of California, 1931-1932. Gouache, 15¾ x 11¾". Lent by the artist. (Plate page 94)

*Bartolomeo Vanzetti and Nicola Sacco, 1932. Gouache, 10½ x 14½". The Museum of Modern Art, gift of Mrs. John D. Rockefeller, Jr. (Plate page 94)

SHEELER, Charles. American, born 1883.

Lady of the 'Sixties (Mrs. Juliana Custer), c. 1925. Oil on canvas, 24⅛ x 13⅞". Collection Mrs. Willard Burdette Force, New York.

SIQUEIROS, David Alfaro. Mexican, born 1894.

*Self-Portrait, 1939. Duco on board, 18 x 24½". Pierre Matisse Gallery, New York. (Plate page 125)

SLOAN, John. American, born 1871.

*Yeats at Petitpas (Van Wyck Brooks, John Butler Yeats, Alan Seegar, Mrs. John Sloan, Celestine Petitpas, Robert W. Sneddon, Anne Squire, John Sloan, Fred King and Mrs. Charles Johnston), 1910. Oil on canvas, 26 x 32". The Corcoran Gallery of Art, Washington, D. C. (Plate page 46)

SORIANO, Juán. Mexican, born 1920.

María Asúnsolo, 1942. Oil on canvas, 56 x37". Lent by the artist.

SOUTINE, Chaim. French, born Lithuania 1884.

*Mme. Marcel Castaing, c.1928. Oil on canvas, 39⅜ x 28⅞". Collection Miss Adelaide M. de Groot, on extended loan to The Museum of Modern Art. (Plate page 89)

SOYER, Moses. American, born Russia 1899.

David and Dog (the artist's son), 1939. Oil on canvas, 42 x 25". The Macbeth Gallery, New York.

SOYER, Raphael. American, born Russia 1907.

*The Artist's Parents, 1932. Oil on canvas, 26 x 28". Lent by the artist. (Plate page 111)

*Self-Portrait in the Second Year of the War, 1941. Oil on canvas, 15 x 10". Associated American Artists, Inc., New York. (Plate page 111)

SPEICHER, Eugene. American, born 1883.

*Katharine Cornell as Candida, 1925–26. Oil on canvas, 84 x 44½". The Museum of Modern Art, gift of Miss Katharine Cornell. (Plate page 91)

A. Conger Goodyear, 1942. Oil on canvas, 36⅝ x 31⅛". Lent by the Trustees of The Museum of Modern Art.

SPIRO, Eugene. German, born 1874.

Albert Einstein, 1941. Oil on canvas, 35 x 28½". J. B. Neumann, New York.

STEIG, William. American, born 1907.

Heart of Gold (Julian Levi), 1942. Pearwood, 11⅜" high. The Downtown Gallery, New York.

STELLA, Joseph. American, born Italy 1880.

St. Peter (Pietro Anselmo), 1929. Oil on canvas, 10¾ x 8". M. Knoedler and Company, Inc., New York.

143

STETTHEIMER, Florine. American.

Marcel Duchamp and Rose Selavy, 1923. Oil on canvas, 30 x 26". Lent by the artist.

*My Sister, 1923. Oil on canvas, 40 x 26". Lent by the artist. (Plate page 80)

STIEGLITZ, Alfred. American, born 1864.

Alfred H. Maurer, 1912. Photograph, gaslight print. Lent by the photographer.

Marsden Hartley, 1915. Photograph, gaslight print. Lent by the photographer.

John Marin, 1920. Photograph, Palladio print. Lent by the photographer.

TAMAYO, Rufino, Mexican, born 1899.

Pretty Girl (the artist's sister, Debora), 1937. Oil on canvas, 48 x 36". Collection Mr. and Mrs. John Rogers, Jr., New York.

TCHELITCHEW, Pavel. Russian, born 1898. Now in U. S. A.

*Joella Lloyd, 1937. Gouache, 23⅜ x 19⅜". Collection Miss Agnes Rindge, Poughkeepsie, New York. (Plate page 103)

Joella Lloyd, 1937. Silverpoint, 18⅞ x 12⅝". Collection Miss Joella Lloyd, New York.

*Lincoln Kirstein, 1937. Oil on canvas, 44 x 36". Collection Lincoln Kirstein, New York. (Plate page 118)

TEBO. Mexican, born 1916.

The Mother (the artist's mother), 1937. Oil on cardboard, 9 x 6⅛". Lent anonymously.

VAN DONGEN, Cornelis T. M. Dutch, born 1877.

*E. Berry Wall, 1938. Oil on canvas, 39¼ x 28¾". Carnegie Institute, Pittsburgh, Pennsylvania. (Plate page 106)

VILLON, Jacques. French, born 1875.

Walter Pach, 1932. Oil on canvas, 16⅛ x 12⅞". Collection E. Felix Shaskan, New York.

VUILLARD, Jean Edouard. French, 1868–1940.

*The Painter Ker-Xavier Roussel and his Daughter, c.1900. Oil on cardboard, 23 x 21". Collection André Weil, New York. (Plate page 40)

*Théodore Duret, 1912. Oil on wood, 37 x 29¼". Chester Dale Collection, New York. (Plate page 43)

WATKINS, Franklin C. American, born 1894.

*Thomas Raeburn White, 1940. Oil on canvas, 35¼ x 45". Collection Thomas Raeburn White, Philadelphia, Pennsylvania. (Plate page 116)

*The Misses Maude and Maxine Meyer de Schauensee and Muffin, 1941. Oil on canvas, 50 x 40⅛". Collection Mr. and Mrs. R. Meyer de Schauensee, Devon, Pennsylvania. (Color plate facing page 116)

WEBER, Max. American, born Russia 1881.

*Self-Portrait, 1928. Oil on canvas, 18⅛ x 16¼". Lent by the artist. (Plate page 88)

The Artist's Son, 1930. Oil on canvas, 16⅛ x 13¼". Lent by the artist.

WEIR, J. Alden. American, 1852–1919.

Albert Pinkham Ryder, c.1902. Oil on canvas, 24 x 20". National Academy of Design, New York.

WESCHLER, Anita. American.

José Limon, 1940. Artificial stone, 12" high. Lent by the artist.

WHISTLER, James Abbott McNeill. American, 1834–1903.

Arrangement in Flesh Color and Black (Théodore Duret), 1883. Oil on canvas, 76⅛ x 35¾". The Metropolitan Museum of Art, New York.

WHITNEY, Gertrude Vanderbilt. American, 1877–1942.

Barbara (the artist's daughter), 1913. Bronze, 20½" high. Collection Mrs. G. McCullough Miller, Westbury, Long Island, New York.

WOOD, *Grant. American, 1892–1942.*

*American Gothic (Mrs. Nan Wood Graham, the artist's sister, and Dr. B. H. McKeeby), 1930. Oil on beaverboard, 29⅞ x 25″. The Art Institute of Chicago. Friends of American Art Collection. (Plate page 99)

YOUNG, *Mahonri. American, born 1877.*

Alfy (Alfred H. Maurer), 1902. Sanguine, 9¼ x 5⅞″. Lent by the artist.

Alfy (Alfred H. Maurer), 1903. Etching, 5¼ x 4½″. C. W. Kraushaar Art Galleries, New York.

*Alfy (Alfred H. Maurer), 1904. Patined plaster, 14⅞″ high. Lent by the artist. (Plate page 77)

ZADKINE, *Ossip. Polish, born 1890. Now in U.S.A.*

*André Gide, 1942. Original plaster, 25⅜″ high. Lent by the artist. (Plate page 121)

ZORACH, *Marguerite. American.*

The Family of John D. Rockefeller, Jr., at their summer home, Seal Harbor, Maine, 1929–1932. Tapestry, 55 x 67⅞″. Collection Mrs. John D. Rockefeller, Jr., New York.

ZORACH, *William. American, born Russia 1887.*

*Mrs. William Zorach, 1924. Pink marble, 18¾″ high. Lent by the artist. (Plate page 97)

ZORN, *Anders. Swedish, 1860–1920.*

Reading (Mr. and Mrs. Charles Deering), 1893. Etching, 9⅜ x 6¼″. The Art Institute of Chicago.

BIBLIOGRAPHY

By BERNARD KARPEL

This list of books and articles is obviously suggestive rather than exhaustive insofar as a bibliography of portrait literature can reflect the point of view of the exhibition. The student of portraiture is referred to the bibliographies in nos. 8, 30 as well as to the reference sources at the end. In addition to the items marked *, many monographs and magazines dealing with the artists represented in the show are to be found in the museum library.

The bibliographical form is modelled upon that used by the Art Index. *Sample entry for magazine article:* BURY, ADRIAN. Who's who in British portrait painting. il (pt col) London Studio 16 (Studio 116): 71–82 Ag 1938. *Explanation:* An article by Adrian Bury, titled Who's who in British portrait painting, containing illustrations part of which are colored, will be found in the London Studio, v.16, p. 71–82, August 1938.

ABBREVIATIONS:
* In the Museum of Modern Art Library.
Ag August, ch chapter, col il colored illustration(s), cop copyright, D December, ed editor, F February, front frontispiece, il illustration(s), incl including, Jy July, Mr March, My May, N November, no number(s), O October, p page(s), pt col part colored, pl plate(s), S September, ser series, supp supplementary, v volume(s).

HISTORIES AND SURVEYS

* 1 BENSON, EMANUEL MERVIN. Problems of portraiture. 28p il Washington, D. C., American federation of arts, 1937.
    Contents: Introduction.—The sitter's point of view.—The artist's point of view.—Concerning method and technique.—Photography and the film: their relation to the plastic arts.—Portraiture: its present and future.
    Also printed in Magazine of Art 30: supp. pl-28 N 1937.

* 2 BURROUGHS, ALAN. Limners and likenesses, three centuries of American painting. 246p il Cambridge, Mass., Harvard university press, 1936.
    American modernism, p211–21.

* 3 BURY, ADRIAN. Who's who in British portrait painting. il (pt col) London Studio 16 (Studio 116):71–82 Ag 1938.

4 HAVELAAR, JUST. Het portret door de eeuwen. 287p incl il Arnheim, N. V. van L. Slaterus' uitgeversmaatschappij, 1930.
    De negentiende eeuw, p231–71.—*Het heden,* p273–83.

* 5 LANGE, ELEONORE H. Portraiture through the ages. il Art in Australia ser4, no1:10–12 Mr-My 1941.

6 LEE, CUTHBERT. Contemporary American portrait painters, illustrating and describing the work of fifty living painters. 110p incl il New York, William Edwin Rudge, 1929.

7 REID, FRITZ. Das selbstbildnis. 159p il Berlin, Die Buchgemeinde, 1931. (Die Buchgemeinde. Jahresreihe 1931–32, bd.3)

8 WAETZOLDT, WILHELM. Die kunst des porträts, mit 80 bildern. 451p Leipzig, Ferdinand Hirt & sohn, 1908.
    Psychologie der selbstdarstellung, p309–414.—*Literaturnachweise,* p417–28.

9 WALDMAN, EMIL. Das bildnis im 19. jahrhundert. 300p incl il (pt col) Berlin, Propyläenverlag, 1921.

CRITIQUES AND ESSAYS

10 ABBOTT, HAROLD. Problems of the portrait painter. col il Art in Australia no75:13–18 My 15 1939.

*11 BARNES, ALBERT COOMBS. The art in painting. 560p il New York, Harcourt, Brace and company, 1937 cop1925.
    Portraiture, p270–77.

12 BENDER, P. Wirklichkeit und wahrheit im porträt. il Die Kunst 79:45–54 N 1938.

*13 BLANCHE, JACQUES ÉMILE. Faces: portraits by Degas. il Formes no12:21–3 F 1931.
Commentary on the nature of 19th and 20th century portraiture.

*14 CALAS, NICOLAS. Confound the wise. 275p il New York, Arrow editions, 1942.
The salutary image, p191–231.

*15 Du BOIS, GUY PÈNE. Portraits of women [from romanticism to surrealism, Museum of French Art] il The Arts 17:343–5 F 1931.

16 FISCHKIN, ROSE MARY. Portraits of artists. il American Magazine of Art 16:528–32 O 1925.

*17 FURST, HERBERT. Portrait painting, its nature and function . . . illustrated with 166 reproductions of portraits. 156p London, John Lane, 1927.
Partial illustrations: Different reactions to the same sitter (pl.XX).—Modern treatment of light (pl.XXX).—Modern emotional and intellectual design (pl.XLVIII).—Modern psychological portraiture (pl.XLIX).

18 GEORGE, WALDEMAR. Masks or faces; the portrait in the history of art. il Apollo 13:271–81 My 1931.

*19 GORDON, JAN. "Psychologics" in portrait painting. il (pt col) London Studio 22 (Studio 122):153–65 D 1941.

*20 GRAHAM, JOHN D. System and dialectics of art. 154p New York, Delphic studios, 1937.
Question 108: What is portrait painting, p108–9.

*21 GREENE, THEODORE MEYER. The arts and the art of criticism. 690p il Princeton, Princeton university press, 1940.
Ch.XVIII: The portrayal of individuals in sculpture and painting, and the rôle of specificity in art, p296–316.

22 GUERLIN, HENRI. Le portrait, choix de textes précédés d'une étude par Henri Guerlin. 174p il Paris, Henri Laurens, 1936 (L'art enseigné par les maîtres).
Ce qu'ont écrit, dit, pensé, artistes et écrivains, sur la technique des arts.

*23 LAMBERT, R. S., ed. Art in England. 150p incl il Harmondsworth, Middlesex, Penguin books ltd., 1938 (Pelican books).
What is a good portrait, by John Steegman, p28–32.

24 MAUCLAIR, CAMILLE. Le problème de la ressemblance dans le portrait féminin moderne. Revue Politique et Littéraire 39:751–5 ser4 1902.

25 PHILLIPS, CLAUDE. Dramatic portraiture. il Burlington Magazine 8:299–315 F 1906.

*26 Portraits of psychotics. il Magazine of Art 30:485–9 Ag 1937.
Contents: 1. Art and psychiatry, by Gertrude E. Benson.—2. Psychological interpretation, by Dr. Ernest Schachtel.—3. Biographical note on the artist, Gertrud Jacob.

27 SLATER, FRANK. Adventuring into portrait painting. il (pt col) The Artist 18:7–8 S 1939.
The mental outlook of the painter, including a comparison of Sargent and Sickert.

*28 WATKINS, C. L. Pictures of people. il American Magazine of Art 26:498–510 N 1933.

*29 WATSON, FORBES. Uncommissioned portraits. Magazine of Art 33:665 D 1940.

PICTORIAL WORKS

30 GOLDSCHEIDER, LUDWIG. Fünfhundert selbstporträts von der antike bis zur gegenwart (Plastik, malerei, graphik). 526p incl il (pt col) Wien, Phaidon verlag, 1936.
Einige literaturangaben, p51–2.
English translation by J. Byam Shaw: Five hundred self portraits. Vienna, Phaidon press, 1937.

31 *MARIA LANI.* 22p plus 52 pl incl front Paris, Éditions des Quatre Chemins, 1929.
Fifty-two portraits of Madame Lani in many media. Essays by Jean Cocteau, Mac Ramo, Waldemar George.

*32 Portrait painters. il (pt col) Life p46–48 F 3 1941.

*33 *STRASSER, ALEX.* Immortal portraits, being a gallery of famous photographs. 149p incl il New York, Focal press, 1941 (Classics of photography).

*34 *VERVE,* the French review of art. no5–6 Jy-O 1939.
Special portraits number.

35 Who will paint your portrait? il (pt col) Town & Country p62–71 D 1939.

REFERENCE SOURCES

36 *AMERICAN LIBRARY ASSOCIATION.* Portrait index . . . edited by Wm. Coolidge Lane and Nina E. Browne. Washington, Gov't printing office, 1906.
Index to approximately 120,000 portraits of 40,000 subjects contained in books and periodicals published up to 1904.

37 *FRICK ART REFERENCE LIBRARY.* [Portraits card catalog] [New York, 1942].
A current file of approximately 300,000 photographs and clippings, of which a large proportion are portraits. Indexed under artist, subject and collection.

38 *SINGER, HANS WOLFGANG.* Allgemeiner bildniskatalog. 14v. Leipzig, Karl W. Hiersemann, 1930–36.

39 _____ Neue bildniskatalog. 5v. Leipzig, Karl W. Hiersemann, 1937–38.
These catalogs (19v) contain references to more than 100,000 portraits of 35,000 persons.

EIGHT THOUSAND SEVEN HUNDRED COPIES OF THIS BOOK HAVE BEEN PRINTED IN DECEMBER 1942 FOR THE TRUSTEES OF THE MUSEUM OF MODERN ART BY THE PLANTIN PRESS, NEW YORK. THE COLOR INSERTS WERE PRINTED BY THE SPIRAL PRESS, NEW YORK.